MW00610949

Every Little Thing

Reflections on Family, Faith and Friendship

Tracey O'Shaughnessy

GOLD MOUNTAIN
PRESS

Gold Mountain Press

Naples, Florida

First Edition
   11   10   09   08   1   2   3   4   5

GOLD MOUNTAIN
PRESS

Gold Mountain Press
Naples, Florida
To learn more about the author, and to purchase additional books:
www.goldmountainpress.com or
www.traceyosh.blogspot.com

DEDICATION

To Hazel Lynch O'Shaughnessy, who wanted to hear
every little thing.

CONTENTS

LOSS: A TRILOGY

Father Falls Into The Arms Of The Drink

My friend's father drank himself to death last week. It took awhile.

My friend and I have known each other nearly 15 years. And in all that time, I knew her father as one thing: a drunk. A boozer. A sponge.

"What's your profession," the cops ask Rick in *Casablanca*. "I'm a drunkard."

My friend's father was a drunkard. That's how I knew him. Funny how swiftly a moniker is applied in an illness like alcoholism. Strange how easy it is to submerge other qualities, no matter how peculiar, perverse -- or endearing. Without realizing it, I had mentally erased her father. She had been estranged from him since the time I knew him, and although he would come up now and again in conversation -- mostly as the root of her emotional derailment -- I dismissed him. He was a drunk and, what was worse, he was an Irish drunk. A caricature. A parody. A cliché.

I don't drink. Never did. Many of us don't. But the stereotypes of the Irish drunk stalk me. They are familiar ghosts. I know their names.

God curse the drink, we say.

God curse the drink, said my grandmother to her son. She knew. Her husband could knock back a few. A different person when he drank. Promise me you'll never drink, son. Promise you'll never take a drink. I promise, Ma. I promise.

A boy loves his mother. A boy makes good on his promise. But the other son -- the sensitive one -- she never asked. He never made the promise. Never took the oath.

God curse the drink, we say. After my uncle died, we found the bottles. I found them. Up in the attic, in a mound covered by an Army surplus blanket. A mound of gallon jugs, their glassy green eyes looking up at me like insects. The insects that devoured my uncle. In the suitcases. In the closet. Under the bed. His legacy. His final Will and Testament.

God curse the drink, we say.

At the Irish funeral home, across from the Irish church, in the Irish section of town where my friend's Irish father lived, we gather. There's a priest named Reilly and a mortician named Douglas. There are sprays of freckles across alabaster skin. There is red hair. There are dimples. There is a man in a casket. Dead of the drink.

An American flag folded into a snug triangle balances on the lid of the coffin. A Boston College yearbook, replete with names like Dunn and Cronin and Deegan, is opened to the deceased's senior picture. Above, a poster rests on an easel. It is garnished with black-and-white photographs and the satiny, fading color snapshots from one of those Kodak 110 cameras. There is the drunk before the drink bored its way through. He is young and handsome with a thin, wry grin and sparkling green eyes. He is outside an Army tent in Europe. He is beside a son on the golf course. He is inundated with a flock of red-haired, impish children, who alight on his lap. He is young and wavy haired, in a uniform, across which is written, "Our Lady."

An old woman who can no longer see well presses her wet blue eyes against the old photograph and says, "Is that Buddy on the end?" The man whose hand she holds for steadiness says, "That's him."

"God love 'im," she says. "Buddy. What a hot ticket. We had a lot of laughs at Our Lady's. All these years and God, I still miss 'im." The woman shuffles through her own darkness to big-bellied men with thick white hair and tears in their eyes. When I enfold my friend, her narrow frame quakes against my chest and I feel what she feels: the warm, choking seizure of memory that dangled a different life before her. A father with a wry grin and the way to make a little girl laugh. A father who knew just where to tickle. A father who tantalized and charmed and beguiled. Not a father who dissolved into arms of drink and never returned to the embrace of family.

It was easier to hate him.

God curse the drink, we say.

How long does it take to drink yourself to death, I wonder. The rain sloshes against the windshield on the long road back home, and I wonder how resolved you'd have to be. In the end, my friend's father gave up all other nourishment. The drink was his Eucharist. It embalmed him.

At dawn the next day, my friend buries her father. But not her ambivalence. What was so terrible that had to be drowned? What couldn't we replace? Why couldn't you love us more than the drink? Why couldn't you have been something else? Instead of a drunk.

God curse the drink, we say.

The Woman You Never Met

I want to tell you about Dorothy, because Dorothy mattered.

Dorothy was not a friend and not an acquaintance, but in that marginal but magnificent middle that most of us find ourselves in. I met her five or six years ago at the local health club. I was pregnant and miserable. She was old and patient. Ivory-haired and bespectacled, she was a tall woman of medium build who had the attitude of a woman who knew how to stay in the background. Unassuming to the point of diffidence, she had an unhurried serenity dramatically at odds with the frenetic thrum so inevitable in a gym. The rest of us, mothers dashing madly to make the nine o'clock spinning class, working women elbowing each other in front of the mirror, could be harried. Dorothy was measured, a grandmotherly antidote to the manic world.

I was, as I say, not among Dorothy's intimates, but began speaking to her one morning when I spotted her on the recumbent bike, quietly thumbing through C.S. Lewis' *Mere Christianity*.

Lewis is among the major gods in my pantheon, but one is not likely to find him in a gym. To discover him in so improbable a place was a revelation and I told Dorothy so. She began to speak in a lovely, articulate baritone about Lewis' major works and what drew her to him. I remember little in specific about that conversation except that Dorothy spoke with a kind of tranquility that seemed borne of deep reflection, and, more, a sense that she had infused Lewis' brand of faith into her daily life, which was more than I could say.

4

Several weeks later, my assessment was confirmed.

I had received notification from my obstetrician that results from a routine blood test indicated a potential problem with my child. I was then in my third or fourth month of pregnancy and had not known enough about the frequent false positives that accompany these tests. The morning I came into the locker room, my attitude was somewhere between grim and terrified. Dorothy was there, and her pleasant composure, in such contrast to my own agitation, frankly troubled me. I am not sure if Dorothy sensed this, or if she had simply meant to bestow the angel on me earlier. But she paused in the locker room, turned to me and said, "You know, sometimes I give these to people in need or people who might need a little something special in their life." Out of her pocket, she pulled a stone, white, weathered and smooth. On it, in Necco wafer-colored oils, was the image of an angel.

"Have a nice day," she said, and left.

Now I don't think that angel was miraculous. And I don't think it cast a spell. I don't think it was the reason, a few weeks later, my sonogram revealed a healthy baby, or why, several months after that, I held my little boy in my arms. I think, only, that it was a moment of grace from a woman of faith.

Sometime last fall, I got news that Dorothy was fatally ill. A cancer that she had fought successfully some years before, had returned. She was receiving frequent blood transfusions. She would not live much longer.

It is difficult to know what to do in such circumstances, when you are not friend, family, or intimate -- when you are in that squishy limbo between acquaintance and intimate. But I felt compelled to do something. And so I decided to tell the truth.

"Dear Dorothy," I began on an ivory colored note pad. "You may not remember me. But you did something for me when I was in a moment of need and I never forgot it. Dear Dorothy, you made a *difference* in my life that day."

I realized, delivering it with a parcel of cookies and a few books on tape, to the nursing home where she was staying, that I needed to thank Dorothy far more than she needed to hear it. I realized that what Dorothy did for me was a simple gesture of kindness of which I wished I were more capable. I realized too, that what prevents such generosity is often the ridiculous notion that it might seem, well, *silly.* Imagine, to balk at kindness out of sheer embarrassment. Silly.

"Be kind," advised the Egyptian philosopher Philo, "for everyone you meet is fighting a hard battle."

Not long after I delivered my note, on a chilly January day, Dorothy died, leaving a cluster of smooth, unpainted rocks, gathered from the sandy shores of her home in West Barnstable, unpainted. But I still have mine. It is a consolation, and a reminder, that often the most innocuous and gentle of gestures are of the most enduring significance.

Connecticut Mutt Tries Puttin'
On The Ritz

Sam the dog was going to the Ritz.

Not originally, of course. Originally it was just to be my husband and I who were to stay overnight at the prestigious Ritz-Carlton hotel in Boston, which seemed extravagant enough.

But when we learned that the Ritz accepts dogs -- "The chef even makes his own doggie biscuits," we were told -- it seemed churlish not to bring him.

After all, hadn't Sam accepted the indignity of a chenille spread and generic dog biscuits for long enough? Hadn't he suffered the humiliation of the pooper scooper and the effrontery of soggy kibbles in his tap water with a patience that bordered on nobility? Hadn't he been marginalized at dinner parties, offered no more than table scraps and drippings?

Surely, Sam's time had come.

I made the reservation.

And then I panicked.

Though well-schooled in the art of paw-giving, tummy-rubbing, "speaking" and defecating on command, Sam hadn't the pedigree of the patrician dogs who frequent the Ritz. No less than the august standard-bearer of distinguished dogness, Rin-Tin-Tin stayed at the Ritz. Lassie -- good grief! -- Lassie, that paragon of canine courtesy, stayed at the Ritz. And heaven knows how many opera diva's pugs, starlet's schnauzers and pedigreed poodles resided at the Ritz. But here's the rub on Sam: he is a mixed breed. Worse, a pound dog, purloined from the puppy projects where, if not for the salvific adoption by tender-hearted suckers, he would have otherwise lived a priapic life of impregnating every saucy little sheltie who sniffed his hind-quarters.

All week, I suffered from pre-traumatic stress disorder. I kept seeing flashes of Sam humping Joan Collins' bichon frise.

"You're going to the Ritz, Sam," I said, as we sped down the Interstate. Sam looked up at me imploringly and stuck out a beseeching paw. This is Sam's way of saying, "Are we there yet?" Two hours and untold paw pleas later, we drove up to the Ritz-Carlton in my husband's pick-up truck. Here we are: Ellie Mae Clampitt and Jethro Bodine.

"We've got our dog with us," I told the doorman. He was well acquainted with this fact, having been cornered under the awning by a growling, snarling Sam, who picked this moment to turn into Cujo. Sam pulled, he barked, he peed on the boxwoods. I looked for a sewer to disappear into. Sam looked for the pickup. My husband grabbed the rawhide. I saw romantic preconceptions dribble down the curb with Sam's pee-pee.

A dashing chap in a cashmere coat swept by and sneered. I looked at him apologetically and tried to remember the number of Motel 6.

Among the more difficult athletic endeavors I've ever attempted was my stuffing of 80 pounds of robust, agile dog muscle, obdurately opposed to it, through the revolving doors and into the Ritz Lobby, trying all the while to preserve a semblance of decorum. "Act normally," I told my husband, Jethro. Sam foamed at the mouth. When he wasn't foaming, he was woofing. People in uniform particularly aroused Sam's ire. Bell boys checked their insurance policies.

I shuffled to the concierge desk, inching behind the man with the cashmere coat and Louis Vuitton luggage. "I have a reservation," I told the concierge. The man with the cashmere coat looked shocked. He moved his Louis Vuitton behind the desk advisedly. Sam backed into a pillar and offered his paw to my husband. "Are we there yet?"

But getting Sam through the revolving door was nothing compared to getting him into the elevators, which are still run by attentive -- not to mention patient -- elevator operators. One of them bent to pet Sam, which inspired yet more barking. I pulled Sam ferociously but suavely (I thought) by the neck. Jethro shoved Sam's flapping hind quarters with quiet desperation, and Sam dug his (ungroomed!) claws into the carpet and we were in.

Sam seemed delighted to be finally encased in our suite. Our understatedly gorgeous room boasted not only a four-poster bed, which Sam was only too eager to jump on, but two silver-plated dog bowls filled with dog treats and water, which Sam was too nervous to thrust his snout into. Instead, he seemed inclined toward permanently cleaving himself to the back of my kneecaps. Wherever I went, Sam followed. When I sat, Sam sat on my foot. When I rose, his nose cemented to my calves. He panted anxiously. So did my husband. So did I. There we were, three panting, anxious rattled wrecks, enjoying a romantic getaway at the Ritz.

Then the unfortunate moment arrived. We had to eat. That meant we had to leave the room. That meant Sam had the suite to himself.

"Just a quick dinner, Sammy," I said. "We'll be right back."

"Stiff upper lip, Sam," said my husband nervously. "Be a man."

But when we shut the door, Sam wasn't a man. He was a caterwauling, whimpering, crying, colicky infant. He didn't bark. He howled. Howled, the equivalent of doggie Ebonics. "Hurry, hurry," I implored my husband. We sprinted to the elevator, our hands over our ears. My husband actually whimpered. Neither of us can take such displays. "Do you think he'll stop?" said my husband desperately.

"Absolutely," I lied. "He'll curl up on that bed and snooze." Down we went on the elevator, wincing at each other, listening to the wail of Sam fade like a siren as we descended. "He'll stop," I told my husband. He uttered something like a yelp and wiped his brow.

"Isn't this romantic," I asked my husband, as we sat in the cozy embrace of the Ritz Cafe, looking out over Newbury Street by candlelight.

"What do you think Sam is doing now?" my husband asked, playing with his poached halibut.

"Sleeping soundly, I'm sure," I lied, planting my fork in the goat cheese. "By the way, you look handsome tonight, doggie -- I mean, honey."

And so it went, romance foiled by parental anxiety. Well founded, as it turned out. When we returned to our room, Sam's audible imploring had not diminished, though he had grown rather hoarse. Hungry only to clutch him in our indulgent embrace, we found we could not get into the room. We were denied access. We called security, waiting eternally while listening to Sam's audible sniffs and whimpers under the door. Finally, a burly, laconic chap with a Secret Service ear piece and an unflattering dark suit arrived. "Come with me," he said. "Didn't anybody tell you that dogs are not to be left unattended in the hotel," he said.

Oh the ignominy of it all. Indeed, we were not told. Images of hysterical heiresses in flapping silk robes, their hands over their ears, clamoring down the hallway, insisting Sam stop his yapping, calling the front desk in droves, filled my head. I could just imagine the valet saying, "We never should have let them in when we saw that pick-up," and the bell-boy replying, "I knew it was a pound dog."

In fact, the front desk staff, which is enormously accommodating and not the slightest bit condescending, cheerily told us that it was not a problem; only one phone call of complaint was received and it was not malicious. They have a little room for unattended doggies, they explained. Next time we come to the Ritz and go out doors, Sammy can frolic there. No problem, he said. Next time.

Next time, I winced. There would be no next time. Sam had humiliated us. This cuddly canine we'd indulged to a fault, buying him his own L.L. Bean bed with a paw-print pattern and monogramming! This dog had betrayed us with his obstreperousness, howling and baying like a farm animal. To be found out as middle-class Connecticut hillbillies with pedigreed pretensions! Oh, the indignity of it all. Later that night I lectured Sam on etiquette. "Do you think Pekingese do that?" I asked him. He merely jumped into bed with me and snuggled into the space between my husband and me. He let out an audible sigh.

As I drifted off on the four-poster bed, Sam's nose touching mine, his chocolate-brown eyes lapping me up with gratitude, I dreamed of home, of monogrammed Bean beds, chenille spreads and generic doggie biscuits, at ease within my own pack.

Brothers, Sisters Are Forever

My mother-in-law walks, now, with a significant stoop.

She is curled over, like a spring fern, and the walker she uses is a sophisticated thing with hand breaks like those on my old Columbia 3-speed.

She is 87, rheumy-eyed and shaky, with eggplant-colored blotches daubing her lustrous olive skin. A few years ago she gave up driving, and now she takes a senior van to aqua aerobics, and a friend from church picks her up for weekly bridge games.

So when she called, a few weeks ago, and said she wanted to travel to North Carolina, I was a little surprised. Raleigh is a good seven-hour drive from her Atlanta home, and, even with her daughter driving, I was afraid she wouldn't be up for it.

But she had a mission.

Her little brother was turning 80.

And she was not going to miss it.

My mother-in-law was born in an Army hospital in Virginia and spent her girlhood on Corregidor, in the Philippines. Seven years after her birth, her brother, Lloyd, was born; and not long after, their mother died. Perhaps this accounts for her unwavering fidelity to her younger brother, or perhaps it is simply that, between brothers and sisters there is a bond that is as unflappable as it is seldom voiced.

"Take care of your brothers," my mother used to say, storming out the front door in a dramatic whoosh. "Don't let anything happen to them."

I was about 14, and my divorced mother worked by day in some sort of software-selling cubical inferno and spent her evenings singing Sammy Cahn and Johnny Mercer songs in cocktail lounges off Route 128.

The responsibility hit me like a thud and I became a little maniacal, instilling in my little brothers a devotion to discipline and punctilious morality that was probably excessive. (It's not a terrific surprise that one of them is now a special agent for the Drug Enforcement Administration.)

I wasn't taking any chances. This was, as my grandmother frequently reminded me, "blood."

And much blood was spilled in those years by my brothers, one of whom was accident-prone and the other of whom was chronically pugnacious. I remember watching my 10-year-old brother Michael's blood seep mercilessly onto the cream wash cloth I held to his head. He had been cut by a troubled boy who turned out to be schizophrenic, and I had pedaled my jade green bike to the house where I found him bleeding and crying, feeling, for the first time, that I could actually kill someone with my bare hands.

What was that force that tethered us together, even while I screamed at them for taking all the marshmallows out of the Lucky Charms and leaving me with the sawdust-tasting remains? How was it that I would slavishly straighten my brother's pigsty of a room, even though he had drawn his boot through my *Saturday Night Fever* album, defiling my prize LP, and my ghastly musical taste?

On the way to North Carolina, where my mother-in-law and her family will surprise her octogenarian brother, I call my brother -- he of the truculent disco critique. My brother has reached a gnarl in his life, questioning his marriage, his health and his own pursuit of happiness. I have made frequent trips, these last few months, back and forth to his house, going over and over the same rutted emotional terrain. I am taxed and spent, exhausted by his demons and frustrated by my own extinguishable insight.

But still, I call, and I listen, and spit out some odious

platitudes of which I am later ashamed. But you don't draw lines with your brother. You don't stop worrying and you carry this weight around you like a physical organ. You are linked, inextricably and infinitely. His anguish finds its echo in you.

When my uncle-in-law walked into the Crabtree Marriott in Raleigh last week, my mother-in-law braced herself on the oak table and stood up. She turned arthritically as her brother, shocked, took a step back and then embraced her. She had come seven hours for this moment and her red-rimmed eyes grew girlish with glee. We were 20 in that room that night, but, really, there were only the two of them, knitted together at the head of the table, thumbing through curled black-and-white snapshots and pouring each other's coffee.

Brothers and sisters. We hold each other's hands and steal each other's Hot Wheels. We share germs and bicycles and winter coats. We staunch each other's wounds and dry each other's tears. We fight through insults and oversights and even exquisite betrayals.

And in the end, we pour each other's coffee and fetch one another's tea because we are the only ones who know how to serve it with the devotion it demands.

New Mom Sees Her Mother In A New Light

Today is my first Mother's Day. That is to say, it is my first as a mother, and not merely as a daughter, which, I have discovered, is an inappropriate vantage point from which to view motherhood.

As a daughter, I saw my mother largely as a figure of enormous flaws. As a mother, I see her as a woman of veiled sacrifice.

Admittedly, my mother is the last person I would describe as self-sacrificing. But that is because most of what I know about my mother's love is corrupted by the limitations of memory. Such is the poignancy of motherhood. All of the best years, the years of staggering, suffocating love, of a joy that swallows you whole and boggles you with its regenerative power, are lost to the boundaries of memory.

My son will no more remember the giddy enthusiasm with which I reacted when he pounded my chest and called me "Mama" for the first time, than I remember my own mother's. Those episodes are lost to the porosity of memory. As mothers, we can only hope that the feelings of those moments lodge between nerve endings, and under membranes and between the folds of the unconscious.

It's something of a cliché to say that you never understand your mother until you become one yourself, but clichés gain in wisdom what they lack in nuance. The truth is, I see my mother now as never before.

I think that's because for most of us, motherhood is an abstraction. Certainly we see our mothers pouring cough syrup down our flushed throats, holding our heads over the toilet and wiping our eyes of tears, but we can never fully comprehend either their sacrifice or their love. It is too abstruse, too enormous to digest. Like most things of any consequence, it is ineffable. And that is a good thing. Were we to fully understand our mothers' love, as E.M. Forster wrote, we would collapse with grief.

How to describe to my son the delicious swell of love that came when his eyes first met mine, when he lit up with happiness at the sight of me? These sensations, like the feel of his small, mitten of a hand in mine, are as inexplicable as they are wondrous. That he will never fully understand them is part of what W.B. Yeats called "the pity of love." It is what you accept as a mother, and it is a realization of great consequence: It is not important that love be reciprocal; it is only important that it be given.

That is the discrepancy that keeps mothers up late at night, alternately praying and cursing at the phone until they hear that their child is safe, that he is healthy and happy.

The older I get, the more I realize the magnitude of that hope. As a kid, when health and happiness seem as ordinary as dawn or dusk, such states seem so facile, so accessible, that their acquisition seems elementary and a matter of course. "I only want you to be healthy and happy," your mother tells you. And you think, "So what?"

It is not until you are older, and you see youth dealt vicious blows, disease mangling the undeserving, hate eclipsing understanding, that you realize how precious health and happiness are, how estimable their possession. It's what makes every parent suppress a gasp of relief when they read of a drunken car accident killing teenagers, or of a deadly disease vested on a child. "There but for the grace...." they whisper guiltily. Faced with the avalanche of daily calamities of frightening proximity, health and happiness seem inestimable indeed.

I can remember standing with my Nana Pascarella outside of St. Bridget's Church after I had received the sacrament of Confirmation. We were posing for a picture on a little glebe of grass, but instead of looking into the camera's lens, Nana looked at me. She pushed the hair out of my eyes and scrutinized me with such amazement, such pride, such love that it made me uncomfortable. Why, I wondered, was she staring at me like that?

Now that I am a mother, I understand. She was marveling at my destiny. I had survived this far and had not yet been visited by what Hamlet called "the thousand natural shocks that flesh is heir to." That dozens were on the horizon and that little could inure me from them is surely something my Nana knew. But for one moment to revel in my destiny, she seemed delectably grateful. I look back on that photograph now and understand with greater clarity than ever what she felt at that moment. But it took motherhood to make me understand. It took motherhood for me to grasp why we would reserve a day to salute them.

Finding Sanctity In A Lighthouse

Sankaty Lighthouse is at the far east end of Nantucket, just outside of Siasconset, where roses cloak small, gray cottages in an aromatic embrace. The lighthouse sits on a sloping ridge on this long, crescent-shaped island, and beside it sits a lonely metal swing set, whose splintery seats sway creakily in the breeze. In the past, signs led tourists to the stately old beacon, but I notice they are gone this year, as though Sankaty Light, as it is called, is reserved for those devoted enough to know the secret passage through Bayberry Lane, up the slow incline that leads to the crest of Sankaty Light.

I come here every year on my bicycle, usually in the early morning hours when Nantucket is asleep and the infamous Nantucket fog blankets the island, lending an air of mystery and nobility to the cobblestone.

It is just early enough to imagine that the island is mine and I am of the island, a native Nantucketer who knows its heather and moors and the tiny footpaths that lead to its still, salty ponds. It is a silly conceit. The island, though pacific and restful in the summer, is harsh and desolate in the winter and demands more of a hearty soul than I have to give. But for the morning, I indulge my fantasy and pedal through the thick, moist gray dawn toward the lighthouse. It is about seven-and-a-half miles through empty, glinting gray paths. Depending on the wind, it can be a rather arduous ride, indeed. But I have with me the symphony of the birds, who have been up longer than I and whose verbosity echoes through the heather and wild roses that overlay the island.

If I push myself, I will reach the lighthouse just as the sun dapples through the fog and paints the harbor a brilliant, saffron yellow.

I make this ride every summer, sometimes twice, which leaves my thighs ruddy with wind and effort, quivering with exertion and memory. It is a devotion of sorts. The lighthouse and the untrammeled streets that lead back into town are a kind of altar at which I pay annual homage. It is a confessional of sorts, a large, airy, imposing penitential pew where I reflect on the year past and make oaths that may dissolve like the fog by this time next year. But I make the passage alone and with hope. Activity holds enlightenment and oceanic opportunity for reflection.

That is what a vacation should be about, not merely indolence, but inspiration. Yesterday, I saw a woman on the beach, talking heatedly into a cell phone, hands on her the hips of her Ann Cole swimsuit, barking out commands into the plastic box. It reminded me of a radio report I recently heard about a man who consults with executives who are workaholics and find that today's technology is their panacea, that drug that enables them to get their fix of work without wingtips or office politics. The consultant makes his living telling such people how to vacation. How to vacation? Good heavens, have we really come to that?

I want to tell the woman with the cell phone to throw it into the cold Atlantic and walk aimlessly along the sloping beach as the tide goes out. It is curious that although we vacation with others, our best moments are those we have alone. Most epiphanies occur not among those we love, but when we are alone with our thoughts, unmoored and unconnected to the outside world. In those alone moments we gather the fortitude and faith that give us the strength to be together.

I know I am close to Sankaty Light when I reach an old wooden houseboat, dry-docked in the sea grass, as if forgotten. Ironically, the boat is called Memory. Nantucket is thatched with bike trails like this one. And I hear from my innkeeper that another such path is being constructed along the road to Polpis and Quidnet, which will link up with the path from 'Sconset, providing a long and intense ride for masochists like myself.

I greet the news with ambivalence. I am glad for the new path, which will allow me safer passage from 'Sconset back to town. But a wonderful desolation exists in this corner of the island; it is where they grow cranberries and great, green ears of corn and lettuce. Along the pond of Quidnet, regal blue herons lord with majestic silence over their briny pastures. My intrepid riding along the side of this lonely road allows me to glimpse them in their slow, elegant repose. I feel an unjust sense of proprietorship over this area; I can't help it, I don't want it to be shared. Silly, I think, and futile. But silliness and futility are what vacations are all about.

As it turns out, I am not alone on the road to Sankaty. I see mothers with strollers, a few gangly runners and a biker or two. All of them are headed to the lighthouse; it is a marker, a touchstone. It is like a child's game: go up, touch the lighthouse, run home. This beacon is the turning point of one's constitutional.

For the most part, lighthouses like this one have been stripped of their romance; no longer is there a hope of a human inhabitant stoking tea inside, offering shelter, succor and clipped conversation. Today, Sankaty Light, like most lighthouses, is computerized, and emits a pulsating, mechanized heartbeat that, nevertheless, inspires a satisfying serenity. And so all of us are mesmerized and attracted to it.

We all need a beacon of this sort. Perhaps it is to remember that there is an end to the road, or that there is an eternal candle; that there is always an always. I think about the early morning journey all of us have taken to the lighthouse. Like monks with their matins, we all pray silently to the same God, but each of us gathers from him a different sort of inspiration. Perhaps it is not so bad that a different bike path will extend to the lighthouse. All of us need such a touchstone.

More importantly, we are hungry for the long and lonely road that leads to it. We will need to revisit it often, in our memories when days are less sunny and auspicious than this.

A French Lesson We Can Surely Use Here

The city of Tours is, like most French cities, encrusted with history. The past saturates this place, soaking it with heavy Romanesque architecture, menacing Gothic plumes and the elegant symmetry of classicism. Tours, like all of France, is a coral reef. Centuries cling to it, embedding themselves on the luxuriant, rich soil that hugs the River Loire and affixing themselves to the cold limestone castles furry with moss.

Tours is not a big city, nor necessarily an important one. It is not much bigger than Waterbury and, like Waterbury, its best days are behind it. Centuries ago, back in the days when Frances I, Henry II and Catherine de Medici cloaked the Loire Valley with chateaux and collusion, Tours was a vibrant battleground of pleasure and royal benevolence. It was here, back in 732, that Charles Martel, master of the Frankish kingdom, halted the advance of the Moors into France, setting the stage for the Carolingian Empire.

All of that was *autrefois*, as the French like to say; literally, "another time," or "long ago." Since then, this cobbled city of about 130,000 has swollen and contracted like the levels of the river that nourishes it. It is now largely a center of commerce, the new regime. Banks nestle against Gothic naves, and flying buttresses umbrella over insurance firms. But along the cobbled quays of the Loire, men with faces like withered apples launch their lines into the capricious current, hoping for a nibble, as they have for hundreds of years.

Tours is a stop on my pilgrimage home to Angers, the Loire Valley city where I lived and attended school in 1983. I am on my way there to see the adoptive parents I loved and to whom I owe much. It is a retreat into the past for me, a burrowing into memory, to that time when I was unfettered by mortgages and mutual funds and could survive on a baguette and a round of Camembert.

At the Quatre Saisons, a tidy, spacious restaurant that sits snugly embraced by one of the town's circles, I sponge the seeping yoke of my omelet *fromage* with my pain, and drown in the lyrical conversations gurgling around me. Meals take time here, and the restraint pleases me. Earlier in the day, I had gone to one of the growing, but still archaic, fitness clubs in the city, where I was chagrined to learn that you can escape the United States, but you cannot escape Britney Spears.

The din of the techno-talent clattered clumsily through the cramped gym. Down the street, a McDonald's does a robust business, while in the next city, Blois, a "Brico Depot" assures the aspiring home refurbisher that "you can do it." The kiosk in the town center advertises the film, "Rachroche," the French title for Diane Keaton's "Hanging Up," and, in the worst offense of all, Air France shows the film "Vatel," with Gerard Depardieu as the 17th century steward of festivities for the rich.

The film is set in France, but all the actors, including Depardieu, speak English, a growing trend in French cinema, which is acquiescing to the insatiable French appetite for the English tongue.

At the Quatre Saisons, the couple next to me inform me that they have been to the United States many times and, with few exceptions, have enjoyed it. The gentleman is in business, and has noticed an increasingly raw competitive spirit in American businessmen. "They are the winners of the Cold War," he explains. "And they know it."

His wife assents but is shocked to find out what Americans do not know. She tells of the time, while in a saloon in Arizona, she was asked where she was from.

The interlocutor was unaware that Paris was in France and equally ignorant as to the location of France itself. It shocked Madame, but not as much as the young law student she welcomed into her home a few years later. The exchange student, who attended Phillips Exeter Academy and possessed exemplary credentials, dismissed the Roman Empire as mythology. Latin was never spoken, the law student asserted, and the Romans were fairy tales, like something out of the Brothers Grimm.

I feel my head drop to my chest. How do I explain this ignorance? How do I explain to this woman that American students are tested to death on their ability to take tests, completely oblivious to knowledge? How do I explain to her that in the United States you are given the option for everything except seriousness? I cannot account for it any more than I can account for the French hunger for Britney Spears or Big Macs.

It is still light when I leave the Quatre Saisons. Dusk takes its time in France, and along the boulevard in Tours, the couples promenade. The boutiques have been locked for hours, but the cafes cater to the lovers and the loungers long after dark. In this city, blemished like most of Europe with pustules of American culture, the French have a monopoly on just what eludes us in the United States. This city, which most Americans don't know and others couldn't place, knows how to stay alive.

We may have spewed the exhaust of American culture into the French atmosphere, but we have yet to export our unique ability to demolish our cities.

A city like Tours doesn't need a mall. It doesn't need a civic center. It doesn't need a spokesman dressed in a silly cape or a slogan as daft as it is ineffective. It is a city not much bigger than Waterbury, and perhaps not even as clever. But it caresses its visitors and seduces them to its broad, clean boulevards and cozy, crepuscular alleys.

It has endured the Vikings and the Moors, the Black Death, the English and the Nazis. It will endure the pestilence of American culture just as effectively.

Some day, perhaps, a wiser urban master may look across to cities like Tours and find therein the secrets to resurrecting cities like Waterbury. Then we may understand what Tours understood long ago: There are limits to the number of hills to which you can flee. Sooner or later, you have to hunker down and build on what you've got.

Privileged And Plain Alike
Will Miss McGrory

When you went to dinner at Mary McGrory's house, it was a good idea not to bring your appetite.

The food was dreadful.

But if you were fortunate to be summoned to the syndicated columnist's Washington, D.C., condo, you were in for terrific conversation.

And it didn't hurt if you could sing.

Mary McGrory, the unabashedly liberal *Washington Post* columnist who died at 85 last week, was my cousin. Don't ask how we were related; I really have no idea. Neither, I suspect, did she. But when I was working as a reporter in Washington and told her that I was related to the Kirbys and therefore to her, she invited me to one of her renowned Sunday night suppers.

I was, of course, terrified.

It was not simply that McGrory was a celebrated columnist and I was a mild-mannered community newspaper reporter. It was not simply that the Kirbys told me she was a complete snob who had an apartment at the Watergate (only half of which turned out to be true). It was that McGrory's steadfast political opinions were only matched by a withering intellect, which was rooted in a vigorous classical education.

My terror was well-placed. Mary did not suffer fools gladly or well. She was not warm. She was not fuzzy. She could write with breathtaking lyricism about daffodils in Washington, the squirrels brazenly exhuming her garden bulbs, or the funeral of John F. Kennedy, but put the spoons on the wrong side of the dessert plates and she could impale you with an acid rebuke.

In his memoir, former *Post* editor Benjamin C. Bradlee wrote of having the privilege of carrying McGrory's bags on the campaign trail. It was an honor columnist David S. Broder also would enjoy. Even in her middle years, moving from a book critic to a columnist at the old, long-lamented *Washington Star* that she deeply loved, she emerged as a scathing critic who could accomplish that genuine Irish trick: To tell someone to go to hell and have him look forward to the trip.

As Marjorie Williams wrote in the *Post* on Sunday, hers was "a souffle of surpassing grace packed with raisins of brutal insight."

Mary was related to me on my maternal grandmother's side. She grew up in the Roslindale section of Boston and attended the elite Girls' Latin School and Emmanuel College. She got her start at the *Boston Herald-Traveler* before moving to the Star as a book reviewer in 1947. Told in 1954 to cover the Army-McCarthy hearings as if she were writing to an old aunt, she began to develop the literary journalism that became her trademark. U.S. Sen. Joseph McCarthy was little more than "an Irish bully," a type with which she was familiar.

She would skewer such types with an opulent lance for nearly 50 years.

The dinner to which I was invited was a little like being invited to an old Irish parlor, except that everybody there was either a diplomat, foreign correspondent or *Post* news editor. The repast featured franks, beans and Boston brown bread, a menu even my mother found appallingly downscale.

But, as with so many Irish dinners, the real sustenance was in the entertainment. After grabbing a dish, buffet-style, in her dining room, we were instructed, not invited, to proceed to the living room. There, Mary presided like a hostess-cum-headmistress, prodding us to get up and sing.

So, here was I, apprehensive that I would be quizzed on Herodotus, only to find myself a contestant on "The Gong Show."

To my surprise, the guests obligingly complied. Mary's devoted old cronies from the *Star,* Gert Cleary and Liz Acosta, who volunteered with Mary at the St. Ann's Infant and Maternity home in the district, started things off. Acosta generously began with "Why Can't A Woman Be More Like A Man," from "My Fair Lady," a bureau chief from the *Post* recited Yeats, and the Irish ambassador's wife did a jig to a campaign manager's percussive piano.

It was a tribute to Mary's graciousness that she did not ask me to perform, although she knew my mother was a singer. I was invited twice more to that strangely imposing and intimate place, and each time it was the same. Mary kept her distance, a countess in her own court, indulged and indulgent.

As far as I knew, all of those assembled were Democrats; she had an almost allergic reaction to Republicans. She hated war and despised hypocrisy, and she wrote with such literary elegance that even if you disagreed with her, you wanted to thank her for enrapturing you with her elegant prose.

During the Reagan administration, she wrote with palpable regret about the public's growing apathy for politics. "I have begun to wonder," she wrote, "what people care about, or if they care at all."

Mary and I were not close. We exchanged notes about twice a year. When I wrote about her beloved Jane Austen (an affection for whom we shared), I would unfailingly send her a copy. She always wrote back with generous, if concise prose. In her later years, she was encouraged by my marriage and the birth of my son, and I detected in her warm remarks a hint of remorse. Mary never married or had children and had, by the end of her life, lost many of her oldest friends. In a town built on phony friendships and marriages of convenience, she loved with a depth and fidelity that, like her erudition on the news pages, is a hallmark of another era. I suspect the loss of such friends affected her indelibly.

Last year, Mary suffered a stroke, which, as Broder wrote, "left this marvelous writer, never at a loss for the right word, with a tongue that will not obey the commands her brain sends."

It was a punishment too ironic in its severity.

Now her tongue is as silent as her pen, and newspapers, and the coarsening culture in which they exist, are destined not to see her like again.

Happy Days Are Here Again,
You Can Buy It Bottled

Shout Hallelujah, I just got Happy.

Happy is the new fragrance by Clinique, advertised by a model kicking the blues away, looking like she just took a fistful of St. John's Wort with a Prozac chaser.

Happy is advertised on television with a model dancing to Judy Garland 's rendition of "Get Happy," Garland's last song for Metro Goldwyn Mayer, which made her famous, but not happy. In fact, despite embalming herself in Joy every night, Garland never really got happy herself, which didn't stop Clinique from naming their new fragrance Happy.

I was actually happy to get Happy, having assumed that happiness was something like clear skin and white teeth that would forever elude me. I thought I would have to settle for splenetic, saturnine, or, if I was lucky, engagingly wry. My suspicions were confirmed some months ago when researchers reported that there was a set point for happiness, just as some say there is for weight. Depending where you fall on the scale, this could mean you would forever be thin and blissful or fat and miserable. Wherever your set point, rest assured: Things will never get much better for you than they are now.

That's why you need Happy, which smells like a cross between orange rind and Lemon Pledge. Happy makes you feel happy, and not only that, but clean. You feel as though you've taken a shower in Tropicana and been buffed to a rosy glow with no tacky residue. It's so fresh, you could see yourself in it. If you're not careful, someone might throw a doily on you and festoon you with Hummels.

Clinique's Happy, as *Elle* magazine attests, marks a trend away from the hollow, hooded, baleful sneer of heroin chic. Heroin chic, says *Elle*, is on the wane, and for that, anybody would have to be happy.

I found it hard to work up a lot of compassion for heroin chic. First, there was the drug angle. Wasn't heroin supposed to make you feel happy? If that is how heroin makes you feel, I'll take cod liver oil with an onion twist any day. And then there was the sympathy problem. How could you feel sympathetic toward a model who was skinnier than you could ever dream of being, had a head of saffron hair but never washed it, straight teeth but never brushed them and scintillating eyes but never opened them?

In addition to looking dispirited, heroin chic made its purveyors look urchin-like and lost, like milk-carton children all grown up. They were bored and depressed and unmotivated, and can you blame them? Their pants don't fit and they have dirty hair.

But the main reason the Droopy Drawers generation (Generation DD) looked so unhappy was they had to face the overwhelming horror of not being able to buy a raised ranch like their parents. How do you go on with gloom like that staring you in the face?

The fashion industry couldn't. All those designers selling despair realized they were precariously close to putting themselves out of business. The problem with despair was that it was so cheap: How much could one charge for frumpy flannel and painter's pants?

Vivid proof that the new generation has embraced happiness was offered in a recent issue of *Harper's Bazaar*. That slender, lemon-haired blonde with the saucy lips and pert nose on the cover was none other than Courtney Love, who once vied with Moms Mabley for the title of Ugliest Person Ever To Become Famous. Courtney Love is now perilously close to looking like Cheryl Tiegs. If she's not careful, she might just land an Ultra

Bright contract. What happened to that disturbing Courtney sneer, that malevolent je m'en fou-ism that made her so lovably hateful? Why, it's gone the way of Roseanne's jowls and Oprah's girth. Now Courtney's not just a mad, unkempt rocker with a bad makeup job, she's one of the Establishment Elite. As such, she has raised her happiness setpoint and given the rest of us something to aspire to.

Courtney Love reminds us that we can only be disagreeable and disheveled for a short time. After a while, either our convictions change or our publicist changes them for us. The next thing you know, we're ordering from Versace and washing our hair in Evian. I have to say, I never liked Courtney Love, but something about her getting a French manicure and a StairMaster makes me really dislike her.

The reason that Courtney and Clinique have become happy is that a survey by the Opinion Research Corporation International showed that nearly 95 percent of American women value happiness over wealth or beauty. (Never mind that for many of those women happiness encompasses both wealth and beauty.) The problem with happiness, as Garland could tell Courtney and the Clinique gang, is that it's so elusive. You just can't get happiness in a bottle. Until now.

"Happiness," Clinique's creative director tells *Elle* magazine, "has become the ultimate product." Never mind what mama told you. You can buy happiness, for only $47.50.

A Life Lost In Memory

When you die at 92, not many people come to your funeral.

You have outlived just about everybody who cared about you; even those few left have silently prayed for your demise, knowing it would be, as they say, The Best Thing.

No, when you die at 92, as my great-aunt Ruth did last week, no one wails and no one sobs, and only a few people dab at their eyes with embroidered handkerchiefs and remember when.

Memory was what Auntie Ruthie lacked. The Alzheimer's disease that wormed into her sharp, witty mind sucked that out of her and left her unable to remember. So it was ironic those who mourned her, chief among them her younger sister -- my grandmother -- mourned her memory, the very thing that had cruelly deserted her.

Alzheimer's disease, the culprit that eventually choked the life out of all her organs, is an insidious disease. It stripped Auntie Ruthie of her memory, but not her ability to cry. Now and again, in the jabberwocky of her dementia, pulling her dress up to her nose or trying to liberate herself from her wheelchair, one precise phrase of truth would come out clean and fresh as a new kitten, and you would know she understood what was happening to her. That would make Auntie Ruthie cry. Not the absence of memory, but the acuity of it.

"What's my name, Ruthie," my grandmother would ask again and again, like a nursery rhyme. My grandmother's overworked, hazel eyes would search out their mirror in

Ruthie's and lock in her gaze, certain if Ruthie saw her, really saw her, she could understand. Over and over again, she would ask Auntie Ruthie her name, desperation rising with each request.

"You're Hazel!" Auntie Ruthie would say, finally, and my grandmother would sigh in relief, "That's right dear," patting Ruthie's gnarled hands and praising God.

Auntie Ruthie's hands could cut through a deck of cards like a hot knife through butter. On the Saturday evenings of my girlhood, when my mother deposited me at my grandmother's pigeon-gray Victorian for the night, Auntie Ruthie, her sister, Auntie Margie, and Uncle Leo, her brother-in-law, would come to play a ribald game of Michigan Rummy at Grandma's kitchen table. Although I was the apple of my grandmother's eye, that kitchen was a sanctum sibling sanctorum on Saturday nights. I was set up in the den with a plate full of chocolate chip bars, a quart of milk and *TV Guide.* "There's a wonderful story on tonight, darlin'," my grandmother would say, pointing to the circled movie capsule in *TV Guide.* Translation: I was on my own.

That was fine with me. It was pleasure enough to peer out through the Venetian blind that striated the bay window, looking for Auntie Ruthie's powder-blue 1968 Mustang. Auntie Ruthie owned and lived in the three-bedroom house in which Auntie Margie and Uncle Leo raised their three children. They were an inseparable triumvirate. They went everywhere in that powder-blue Mustang, with Auntie Ruthie at the wheel, the breeze combing her lush, snowy-white hair.

Legend had it Auntie Ruthie's onyx hair turned "pure white" the day she turned 30. It was part of the myth of Auntie Ruthie and perhaps a way to explain why she -- alone among her nine siblings -- never married.

"She had plenty of fellas, though," my grandmother would say. "Lots of fellas." Even then, the idea of having lots of fellas, but choosing none, piloting oneself through life in a Mustang, had its exotic appeal. Auntie Ruthie, the one who jumped out of the second-story window with an umbrella, the one who was the fastest box-maker in the plant, was deliciously free of responsibilities and devotedly loyal to her family.

"Don't try closing the drapes; we're here," my Auntie Ruthie would say, alighting the front steps smelling of Joy and Aqua Net. "I don't know why I bring you these candies; you're as big as a house as it is," she would say, forcing a box of chocolate-covered cherries on my grandmother.

"Aw, who invited you," Grandma would say. "They're probably poison. Get outta here, or I'll call the cops."

And so it went throughout the evening, as the siblings swapped jibes and pennies in the den. I paid perfunctory attention to the eight-o'clock movie and nodded off to the lullaby of their gentle jokes and hearty laugher.

Today, my brothers, sisters-in-law and I gather together for raucous games of Trivial Pursuit and Tri-Bond. We don't know who wins, but the unfortunate among us who blunders is remembered forever. "What's-a-matter wit chew, ya jack-ahss," we'll say. We tease each other relentlessly, and the slow-witted of the moment is forever at the mercy of our swift, lacerating repartee. One does not live long among the Irish without a fast wit and thick skin.

And on those evenings where there are no hours and no victors, when the sound of our laughter echoes like a symphony along the oak floorboards, I sometimes wonder who among us will fail first. It is the minor key that haunts those nights, the ghost of the Auntie Ruthies and Auntie Margarets that tap on my shoulder, reminding me: Relish these moments; neither they or their memories will last forever.

My grandmother is sustained by these memories now. In her butterscotch recliner, nestled into the same bay window at which I awaited Auntie Ruthie, the memories tick by like the clucking seconds of the Seth Thomas clock on the wall. The memories should warm her now, but they don't. These phantoms from the past come near enough to tease, but not to touch. In such a world, it is easy to think having one's memory erased is perhaps better, in the end, than having it precise enough to yearn.

Will The Real Jane Please
Say Something?

It is a truth universally acknowledged that a single woman in possession of a good mind must be in want of a man.

However little credibility the cheek or accuracy of such a presumption may hold in academic circles, this truth is so well fixed in the minds of the creative forces of Hollywood that the lady in question may consider her virtue shattered.

Such, at least, has been the treatment English literature's first great authoress, Jane Austen, has received on screen.

Her heroines have been prettied up; dumbed down and sexed up, so it shouldn't be surprised that the latest cinematic injustice should take Jane herself as its target.

Jane has been violated.

But not by Tom Lefroy, the dashing blackguard who becomes her One Great Love in "Becoming Jane," the latest cinematic confection about her romantic life. By something far more sinister.

"Becoming Jane" attempts to fill in the blanks -- and there are disturbingly many -- of the early 19th century novelist by suggesting that her prodigious narrative powers were inspired by a great love affair. It's a simplistic, if impertinent, explanation for one of the great riddles of the early novelist: How was Austen (1775-1817), the spinster daughter of an impecunious church rector, able to craft such breathtakingly insightful novels about human nature? How was a largely self-educated woman able to move English literature from the bombastic pretense of Walter Scott and Henry Fielding into the shrewdly observed, impeccably crafted novel of manners and morality that have influenced writers from George Eliot to Toni Morrison?

Austen's six novels, published between 1811 and 1818, are regarded as among the finest in English literature. But the root of Austen's uncanny discernment has proved elusive for critics, most of who have wrestled fruitlessly with the paucity of biographical material about her.

Her sister Cassandra -- and later her niece, Fanny -- destroyed many of her letters, Cassandra because she believed they revealed too much; and Fanny because they revealed too little. "The uneventful nature of the author's life...has been a good deal exaggerated," Austen's great nephews asserted tantalizingly -- then offered nothing juicy as evidence.

"Becoming Jane" attempts to settle the matter by insulting her. Screenwriters Kevin Hood and Sarah Williams suggest that Austen's inspiration was the Irish lawyer Lefroy, who not only spirits her away for a scandalous marriage, but introduces her to Great Literature.

Austen buffs like me can handle the whimsy of an Austen romance. We can handle the preposterousness of the aborted elopement. Some of us can even handle Jane losing her virtue. But to suggest that Jane Austen needed a patronizing tutorial on literature delivered by a man is beyond the pale.

"The idea that Tom Lefroy sparked Jane's brilliance is totally foolish," author Dierdre LeFaye told *The Washington Post*. "She came from a very smart family. By the time she met Tom she was already an accomplished writer."

Indeed, by the time she met him, she had already started three major novels, all before reaching the age of 24. She had read *Tom Jones*, a lusty romp, long before she met Lefroy.

While it's probable that Austen did have more than a fling with Lefroy, it's outrageous to presume she needed him or any other man to ignite her genius.

It's neatly romantic to presume that genius requires a lusty combustion. But most of its practitioners will tell you that it has most to do with sweat and an unnatural proclivity for sitting still for long stretches of time.

What is particularly injurious about this misogynistic interpretation is that Austen sacrificed so much for her art. She lived on a trifling allowance of 50 pounds. She was constantly decamping for this or that wealthy relation because she and her sister could not support themselves. At 27, she accepted a handsome offer of marriage from a man that would have made her the mistress of a large Hampshire estate, able to support her aging parents and spinster sister. But, after a sleepless night, she changed her mind and spent the rest of her life unmarried. More than once, she described her novels as "my darling children," though she lived scarcely five years after their publication. She died at age 41, having earned a meager profit of 84 English pounds and 13 shillings on her novels.

Austen was not the model of integrity that her characters were. She was caustic and catty; by her own admission, beastly and a little bawdy. But she was a woman in complete command of her own powers. She needed no man to light her creative fire. The inference that she does shows how tenacious misogyny is, and how perplexed we continue to be over the powers of the imagination.

Good And Evil Reside Side By Side

In the "freedom summer" of 1964, a young *New York Times* reporter named Joseph Lelyveld went to the Maspeth section of Queens and started knocking.

He had been sent to the blue collar neighborhood to seek out a woman named Mrs. Ryan.

Lelyveld, who would go on to become executive editor of the *Times*, was in Queens on a tip from the celebrated Nazi hunter Simon Wiesenthal, a woman who called herself Mrs. Ryan was, in reality, an infamous death-camp guard, Hermine Braunsteiner, known by prisoners there as the Stomping Mare. She was known for her pitiless selection of women and children for the gas chamber, and for her predilection for whipping women to death, kicking away stools to hang children and stomping old women to death with her jackboots.

It only took Lelyveld two doors to find her. "Mrs. Ryan," he said. "I need to ask you about your time in Poland, at the Maidanek camp, during the war."

"Oh, my God," Ryan said. "You've come."

When was hauled Braunsteiner in to court, becoming the first United States citizen to be extradited for war crimes in 1981, neighbors couldn't believe it. Her husband called the *New York Times* to say his wife was the most decent person he'd ever met. "She wouldn't hurt a fly," he said.

The newspaper that unmasked her reported her death last year, six years too late. She died on April 19, 1999, at the age of 79. She had been freed three years earlier for health reasons by a West German jail that had been holding her for life.

Last month, Gov. Arnold Schwarzenegger considered sparing one of the most notorious criminals of his time. Stanley "Tookie" Williams, was once a leader of the infamous street gang, the Crips, a gang that would shoot you for your shoes.

Although Williams maintained his innocence of the four murders for which he was convicted, more was at issue over his clemency than his probable guilt. The question was not whether he was, in his own words, "despicable;" he was. The issue, according to his supporters, was that he had, Scrooge like, changed. His was a trans formative redemption. And "redemption," he told a newspaper reporter, "is tailor-made for the wretched."

After his sentencing in 1981, Williams became the Magdalene of misanthropes. He wrote children's books, a memoir and the Tookie Peace Protocol, forms for rival gangs looking for a truce.

But there was no absolution for Tookie Williams, just as there was none for Braunsteiner. In Christian theology, mythologized this year in the Hollywood version of C.S. Lewis' *The Lion, The Witch and The Wardrobe*, an innocent sacrifices himself for the sinful and asks the sinful to absolve the wicked among them.

But a courtroom is not a confessional and Christian values seem only to be invoked in politics when they are expediant and the circumstances dire, as in whether a sales clerk wishes you a "Merry Christmas" or a "Happy Holiday." Karla Faye Tucker may have turned away from sin and toward compassion, but how does one reconcile that with the dead whose lives she took with a pick-axe. Can such evil ever be replaced with good? What do we owe the victims? Is it equal to what we owe to "reformed" killers?

In one of the year's most talked about films, "Walk the Line," Joaquin Phoenix, as Johnny Cash, confronts the evil within him with a mixture of self-hatred and desperation.

The man who sang "I shot a man in Reno just to watch him die" was painfully aware of our inherent capacity for evil. In the early days of this country, that innate sinfulness was an accepted facet of our being.

Today, it sounds alternately draconian, or quaint. But as the New Year dawns and resolutions are made and broken, it is perhaps time to reflect on the decency and depravity in all of us. We are not supposed to, of course. In the same way that there are "no bad foods," we are supposed to believe there are "no bad people." But history suggests quite the opposite. Whether people can be bad for a time -- and then good. Or good for a time -- and then bad, remains a matter of philosophy. But most of us, in lesser degrees than the notorious, dangle our toes in both of those streams. We should consider ourselves mighty lucky indeed if it only takes the New Year for us to realize that.

Friend's Departure Stirs Regret

My friend is moving.

"Don't worry," she says. "St. Louis is only 18 hours away."

I'm a New Englander. To me, two hours is an excursion. But my friend is from Portugal, a citizen of the world, really, and has friends sprinkled all over the planet. Compared to Lisbon, St. Louis is right around the block.

"You'll visit," she says.

"Sure!" I say, thinking *not in a million years.*

I have never been very good at feigning indifference. But my friend is so sanguine -- merry, really, that I try to meet her cheeriness with a glibness that is excruciating to carry off.

Behind this affected blitheness is deep disappointment. St. Louis might as well be Timbuktu, as far as I'm concerned. I suspect I'll never see Maria again.

I don't tell her this, of course. Nor do I tell her how much her departure hurts. Nor, unforgivably, do I tell her how much I love her.

Transience is a way of life in the 21st century. It is nowhere near as tragic as it was at the beginning of the 20th century, when my grandfather got on a bus in his Cork, bound for America, the bus turning down the familiar corner of his street with inexorable slowness, taking him away from a place to which he would never return.

Now, of course, we have cell phones and text messages and instant messaging and a whole chimera of technology that insists we are all webbed into one snug neighborhood that has rendered obsolete the tragic tug of loss.

I never believed any of this, perhaps because I am a demandingly intimate friend and require a touch of a hand, a return of a smile, a riveting gaze, and that distinctive scent of a friend when she sits down next to you.

I came to Connecticut 15 years ago, and when I did, I left a dozen souls, all dear to me, in Washington, D.C. Before that, I left my hometown, and everything and everyone I knew. The other day my son, 7, told me he planned to go to Quinnipiac University, only because he could walk to it. "I don't want to go away from home," he says.

I didn't feel that way when I got on an Amtrak train at the 128 Station in Westwood, Mass. My mother handed me my father's Army duffel bag and a foot locker from Sears. "Have an adventure," she said, and I suppose I did. But even now, nearly 30 years later, leaving my hometown has left a lacunae in my heart no cozy cape can fill. Nothing makes up for what was lost.

A part of me is angry at my friend for her enthusiastic farewell. Some nerve. Couldn't she evince a little despair? Some mild, slightly cinematic hysteria? I don't ask for much, but without a little drama, I begin to suspect my friend doesn't care. I begin to suspect she actually looks *forward* to it.

And then I do something that really is beneath me. I begin to enumerate all her failings. Her quarrelsome nature. Her enigmatic, appraising, eviscerating stare. Her terminal tardiness. And, worse of all, a fluency in English that surpasses mine.

None of this assuages my gloom, and only increases my shame. The truth is I am simply tired of losing friends like a snake sheds its skin. This is the third good friend I have lost since moving to Connecticut, and I'm beginning to lose hope. I know young people don't like Connecticut, but it seems a decent enough place to molder into middle age.

At the beach in Rhode Island not long ago, a little boy with sand-filled pants came up to my son and said, "Wanna be my best friend?"

What marvelous audacity, I thought. When in the world did I lose that? It was audacity that led me to Maria, whom I met in an optometrist's office, where she sat reading a French novel. I'm a reticent person, but I can't resist a woman reading a French novel, and it was there she and I began our friendship.

All of that reminds me that it takes a little dash to initiate a friendship, and something like Maria's delicious outlook to maintain one. "My friends are always with me," she says, clutching her heart. "Distance does not exist. Friends are in your soul, my dear."

Maybe this is her buoyant Iberian tonic for disappointment -- so much healthier than my maudlin Celtic brew.

You are right, as usual, my enigmatic friend. You can't miss something that is inside you.

Beachside Memories And Salty Tongues

On a Sunday morning, the sky a soft, robin's egg blue, I took my son north, to Cape Ann in Massachusetts, where I had spent so many summer afternoons as a girl.

My mother came with us, which was only fitting, since it was she who had herded us all into her pea-green Pinto 30 years ago and introduced us to the place. Now she would introduce my son, a 3-year-old with a fascination for sand castles, dump trucks and his "big fat Nana."

My mother was always a beach person. It was one of the many sharp divisions between her and my father. My father was, at best, a lake man, a man who enjoyed the predictable tranquility and dependable grassy estuaries and shady pines the placid pools offered. At the beach, sand lodged between his toes and the sun singed his pale Irish skin. Just to look at the sun, he said, could give him a second-degree burn.

But my mother is half Italian, and her skin soaked up the sun's merciless rays and turned her a honey brown. The ocean's mercurial ways suited her impetuous personality. Like most beach people, she was as impulsive in her flight to the beach as she was indifferent to its weather. Sun was, of course, preferred, but my mother sped to the beach at the first hint of hurricane weather. She stood on the seawall, wrapping herself in my father's old Army jacket, waves lashing against the pier, laughing demoniacally.

"Isn't this wild!" she'd shout over the thundering surf.

My mother took any excuse to go to the beach, but the most frequent was that she had to get out of "this damned

46

house" before it crashed in on her, a common lament, I suspect, for housewives in the `60s. Realizing that trying to induce my father to the beach often unleashed deep divisions between them, she soon gave up her entreaties and instead grabbed her three children, an avocado green cooler and a colonial brown beach bag full of blankets and headed north.

A suburban child will grab any excuse to leave the stultifying boredom of a summer Sunday, and so even though a beach outing meant I would spend the evening slathered in Noxema, my skin the color of strawberries and the texture of sandpaper, I followed my mother with zest.

So up we would go, north on Route 128, my mother singing along with Eydie Gorme and Vic Damone on the radio, my brothers and I fighting over Pop Tarts in the back seat, my father contentedly trimming his hedges at home.

Most of our neighbors were Cape people, devotees of Falmouth and Chatham, heading south to Buzzard's Bay. But my mother found the Cape too placid. She preferred the roiling surf of Gloucester, the flinty, rugged shore of Rockport, just north of Boston. We learned to absorb her enthusiasm for the place, hopping over the pale yellow boulders, finding crabs and desiccated black seaweed in the coves, and horseshoe crabs on the ragged shoreline.

It was easy to imagine ourselves as explorers and inventors in the cave-like seclusion of the rocky inlets. Imagination seemed to flow in there like the tides. And there my brothers and I would be, in our flip-flops and terrycloth cover-ups, launching driftwood torpedoes and clam-shell grenades at each other, while my mother stood sentinel with her transistor radio and tube of Ban de Soleil, telling us to, for God's sake, be careful.

We would stay there until late afternoon, our flesh a speckled Jackson Pollock canvas of crusty gray sand and crimson glyphs. "Alright, kids, that's the ball game," my mother would say, clapping her hands of the sand and folding our Hilton Hotel towels into the beach bag. We would whine a reflexive dissent, tempered only by my mother's assurance that we would all be treated to hamburgers and curly French fries at her favorite clam shack. In the evening, our bellies full and our skin tender to the touch, we would fall asleep in the back seat, our hair clotted with sand, the car redolent of onion rings and the susurration of the car tires rolling on the chalky gray streets.

My mother is older now, but she has not lost her enthusiasm for the beach. In the trunk of her gold Honda, she keeps a lawn chair, beach towel and "trashy paperback novel" just in case the urge should strike.

Wingaersheek Beach, where I played as a girl, is very much the same, its swath of sand framed by Olympian boulders and soft dunes, stretching out along the left bank of the Annisquam River. I take my son there on a postcard perfect day, when the tide is low and the beach is expansive and ripe for castle building.

I sit with him on the hard, damp soil, looking toward the looming boulders, seeing shadows of myself lunging from rock to rock, parachuting in on my brother's cove, running madly away at the first sight of gooey green seaweed.

It is the same and different. I am no longer the girl who cared only about curly French fries and Fanta grape soda. I worry about jelly fish and UVA rays, green flies and $25 parking fees. I think about work the next day and traffic on the ride back. I want to ride through the windy streets of Annisquam and Rocky Neck, picking out my favorite house and imagining my home on an ocean point, as we did with my mother, who appropriated many homes from the cockpit of her Pinto as she sucked down cherry Italian slush.

So many of the dreams I had then have been tempered with time. So many of the people who loved me have died. The fabric of life that I am giving my son seems not as rich as the one in which I grew up. It seems tamer and more careful, duller and more proscribed.

On the ride back through the narrow, sand-dusted streets, my mother tells me about the beach days of her girlhood, when her cousins and aunts would cook lasagna and meatballs for days before, and head to Buzzard's Bay with a caravan of Italian relatives at dawn on a Sunday morning. They would stake their claim to a fire pit. They would set picnic tables with linen (yes, linen, she assures me) tablecloths and sterling silver. Someone would have an accordion or a mandolin. And all day and into the evening, they would eat and sing and swim in the surf. "So carefree," my mother says, shaking her head.

It strikes me how much better those memories sound and how filled with nostalgia my otherwise unsentimental mother becomes.

I look at my son, who has fallen asleep with a sand-clotted dune buggy in his hand and chicken nugget flakes over his plump skin. I wonder what memory he will have of this day, or whether he will remember it at all. I wonder whether it is the quality of the memories or simply the hum of remembering itself that turns us wistful.

His mind sifts through episodes at which I was present but to which I am not privy. He will have his own memories, soft and sweet and even bitter, filled with characters who I know only partly. On this day, I have handed him the raw materials to make his own castles of nostalgia. He may see me there soon, the ghost that led him through these rich estuaries of simpler, carefree days.

Search For Answers Yields
Oceans Of Questions

The limestone is cool and wet beneath my belly. It soaks through my jeans, leaving impressions of powdery beige moss on the denim. Using my chin like a finger, I creep to the end of the slab of rock and peer over, into the abyss.

Seven hundred feet below, the roiling ocean crashes upon the cliffs, spewing frothy white water up the kelp-frosted cliffs. I am at the Cliffs of Moher, on the west coast of Ireland, looking into eternity.

There are no guard rails around me, no fretful sentries, alerting sensors or cautionary signs. There are just these cliffs that drop 650 feet into the ocean. If I stand up, I will get vertigo and that perverse wonder of what it would be like to step off in one slippery, exhilarating leap into serenity. Instead I press myself into this rock and watch the swirling ocean, and the gliding, pollen-like birds that float back and forth over the air currents like dust.

I have come here to untangle secrets. But as I look into the ocean, I realize that I am as far away from the truth as the Atlantic is from the limestone that supports me. I had hoped to find out the reason for my grandfather's 1926 departure from his well-appointed house in Cork to a suburb of Boston in the United States, but what I have found is an eddy of stories that dizzies me still.

On the Aran Island of Inis Mor, a potbellied man with a southern drawl stands next to a pony cart that has taken him to a ruin. He explains to the ruddy-faced cart driver that he has come here to trace his ancestry and the driver lifts his cap off and scratches his feathery white hair and says, "Aye."

This, his face says, is a story he has heard before.

We have all come here to find out where we came from, and what we are looking for is more than dates and dashes etched on tombstones. A million people died here because of the potato famine in the mid-19th century, and if you travel through the jagged mounds of creased rock called the Burren, you will understand why.

The place is a desolate moonscape of a quiet so abject it seems to howl with hunger. At points, the bald gray hills collapse into steps of ocher rubble. In this blistered, scaly place, the roofless remains of cottages materialize like ghosts, and ghosts they are. These are the forsaken tombs that were the homes of the people who tried to scratch a living out of this merciless rock. In the slough of oppression and lost hope that is the Burren, you understand the desperation that led three million Irish to risk the "coffin ships" that brought those who survived to the United States and Canada.

In the car, I finger the brick of brown bread I bought in Kinsale and gnaw at its soft core hungrily. Why didn't you tell me about this, Grandpa?

For that matter, I think, back in his home city of Cork, why didn't anybody ask?

It is from this house that my grandfather's sister, Elma, ran shrieking with her scalded 2-year-old, to Mercy Hospital below. But mercy saved neither the child nor her sanity. For her husband, a former boxer, it was worse. Infected with anger, he fought with a man at work and killed him with his bare hands. He fled Ireland and his wife soon followed. I can see that hospital from here, the same place where they brought my Aunt Kathleen when she miscarried her Protestant husband's child. She died there, riddled with poison from the infected placenta, and her mother, a Catholic, watched from the bridge as her daughter's cortège drove Kathleen to her final resting spot -- a Protestant cemetery.

But about my grandfather, Frank, there is only rumor.

In my cousin Mary's modest home, Lindisfere, I sit on a slip-cushioned sofa and ask were the rumors true about Frank being involved with the Irish Republicans?

Mary wrinkles her hooked nose and says she wouldn't know, nor does her sister Carol. And in that stucco room, I feel my dreams fade. All who were alive during my grandfather's day are dead. And my grandmother never asked him. Or he never told. And what would have gnawed at me in a 1990s marriage didn't faze my grandmother at all. Whatever Ireland was like, and why her husband ever left, was lidded by acceptable secrecy.

I should feel worse about this than I do. I am prone to regret, but in this simple room I feel none. It is enough to hear my cousins laugh, to listen to the trill of their voices as they tell increasingly comical and incriminating stories about one another.

They talk politics as well, and melancholy layers over humor and regret in the sedimentary rock that is Irish culture. I have never met these people before this day. But I swirl into an orbit like a wayward planet, and the cadence of their conversation is so embracingly familiar that there is no doubt that they are family. We may have lost the substance of the stories, but we have lost none of the ardor of telling them. We have nothing but bitter tea and glasses of stout in this room, but we have the language that turns to music in the mouths of the Irish. And we strike the notes and rise to the crescendo and savor the blessing that is the English language and the gift that is using it well.

In the end, I have unraveled nothing. In the end, I am raveled into the web of family. I have picked up the skein and knitted myself into the pattern. It is what will keep me warm when I am far away from them, and still feel their kisses like mist.

Little Boy Has Lost His Handel

I'm *not* doing this.

Not. You understand. Not. I'm not going to be of those push-over parents who indulges their child's every whimpering whim. I'm not going to be camping outside of Toys 'R' Us in the wee hours of the morning, sucking down instant coffee, reading by mag lite, ready to pounce on the next shipment of Power Rangers. Not me, sweetheart. Talk about mollycoddling your kid.

The problem with kids today is they get everything they want. Everything. Now, when I was a kid we knew how to appreciate what we got, which was nothing, but we were grateful for it anyway.

It was with such Draconian temperament that I went into parenthood. Better to have a child suckled on deprivation than wantonly indulged like the simpering pantywaists I see in my town.

That was before Thomas the Tank Engine.

Who can explain the hypnotic effect this cheery blue engine has on the supple minds of toddlers? How to decipher its mesmerizing allure? Ever since Thomas chuffed his merry way into our little yellow house, our son has been under the steam engine's spell. Thomas the Tank Engine, for the fortunate few who have not been initiated into this enchanting cult, is based on a series of stories by Rev. W. Awdry about a depot full of trains, all of whom have personalities that roughly mirror those of your colleagues at work.

Some are huffy. Some are saturnine. Some take credit for the work of others. Some think their diesel is ice cream.

Thomas the Tank Engine is the railroad equivalent of Sociology 101. You can learn an awful lot about human nature watching people transport coal.

Because of that educational component, I welcomed my son's burgeoning enthusiasm for Thomas stories.

Welcomed.

But I swiftly learned the first lesson of parenthood. No salubrious element of childhood cannot be merchandised, marketed and manipulated. And Thomas is no exception. Dozens of Thomas the Tank engine characters, in wood and die-cast, are available for purchase. And we have (gasp) purchased.

And purchased.

And purchased.

Loathe though I am to admit it, we have, at last count, 47 Thomas the Tank engines, from Annie to Stepney and everywhere in between. You might suppose that we had cornered the market on Thomas the Tank engine products, but then you would be underestimating the creative rapacity of Learning Curve, which markets the stuff.

In my defense, apostate Spartan that I am, I will say that my son does not clamor for any other toys. Single-minded as his mother, PJ is a monogamous shopper. It is Thomas and Thomas only all the Thomas time.

And everything was going clickity-clack smooth in our little track-laden universe until the inevitable occurred: one of the trains went missing.

"Where's Handel?" said PJ one fateful autumn afternoon.

"I don't know, PJ. Where did you put him?"

"Handel!" PJ called, "Handel!" He walked the length of the backyard. He clamored under the deck and emerged caked with pine straw and coppery soil. "Handel!" he cried, sprinting through the den, discarding sofa cushions and lampshades in earnest pursuit of his wayward train. And finally, good little Catholic that he is, he resorted to the Prayer of St. Anthony:

-- "Tony, Tony, look around. Something's lost that must be found."

Alas, even celestial intercession couldn't find Handel.

Now in my pre-parental, Gen. Patton-like state, I would have a simple answer to this: Get over it, kid.

But one look into my son's timorous blue eyes, his fleshy pink cheeks and petulant, trusting mouth and I did what every guilt-ridden, overburdened, knucklehead of a modern mother does: I whipped out the Visa card.

Alas! To no avail! Even the Herculean powers of my overburdened yet shatteringly effective credit card could not solve the Handel dilemma. Handel, I learned from my obliging neighborhood toy store, has been retired! Retired, you understand. No longer made, sold, marketed or mass produced. I let my head fall in my hands. "Is there nothing you can do?" I pleaded with the cashier. "Nothing?" She put her hand on my shoulder. "Maybe," she said, "You can try e Bay!"

E Bay! The last resort of the terminally desperate. Why hadn't I thought of it before?

But one click onto e Bay and my ascetic temperament returned. Lots of people had clearly thought of e Bay before I. They had inflated the price of Handel to roughly the equivalent of a Van Gogh. Forget it! I huffed, coming to my senses. PJ will learn the lesson of loss. He will learn that you cannot get everything you want in this miserable world. He will learn that you must take care of your things.

Thus resolved, I parried the frequent impassioned requests for the return of Handel. "You'd better take care of your things, PJ," I said sternly, not meeting his gaze.

Until one night, snuggled close in bed, we finished the story "'Twas the Night Before Christmas."

When the book was tucked away and PJ snuggled into his crib, he looked up at me and said, "Will Santa bring Handel back to me?"

THAT'S IT!

I would pay any price, bear any burden, climb any mountain, ford any stream, invoke every cliche.

For, after all, how can there be Christmas without Handel?

Warming To A New Pope

At the dawn of the 17th century, the Renaissance master Botticelli unveiled a painting known as *The Mystic Crucifixion.* It's a creepily evocative image of a slingshot-wielding angel screaming out of the blackened heavens, clutching a tiny lion, ready to set Florence aflame.

Well, Florence deserved it, but not nearly as much as Rome, which was then toxic with randy, grasping popes and riven with ecclesiastic dissension. The angel is said to represent the notorious Girolamo Savonarola (1452-98), of "bonfire of the vanities" fame, a rather sanctimonious Dominican intent on purifying the debauched church. At the foot of the cross, the ever-repentant Mary Magdalene, representing the Catholic Church, clutches the cross, as the wolf of clerical vice flees from under her robe.

The painting hangs inside the Fogg Art Museum at Harvard, just a stone's throw from the epicenter of the priestly pedophilia crisis in Boston. I was queerly transfixed by the painting, not least because I was looking at it only days after Pope Benedict XVI had met with victims of the abuse, telling them that it was important that "those who have suffered be given loving pastoral attention."

Pastoral attention was the central motif in the pope's 5-day visit to the U.S., a visit that many Catholics found invigorating and others found wanting. Today's church may not be as degenerate as that of the 16th century, whose tales of simony, incest and lechery are a grotesque stain of Catholic history. But the clergy scandal counts 13,000 victims, netted 5,300 priests and cost the church $2 billion. Catholics may not need another Savonarola -- ultimately hanged and burned in 1498 -- but it needs something. The question for the devout, and I count myself among them, is: Is Benedict it?

It may be that the level of turpitude by these priests and the emotional evisceration were too grave to salvage the faith of the victims. As one of the victims, Olan Horne, of Lowell, Mass., told *The Boston Globe*: "I asked him to forgive me for hating his church and hating him. He said, 'My English isn't good, but I want you to know that I can understand you, and I think I can understand your sorrow.'"

That's a moving testament to Benedict's personal sorrow over the crisis, a long awaited and theatrical act of penance, from a church that is no stranger to spectacle.

Only one out of every four Catholics born to the religion remain faithful to it today. Were it not for the influx of Hispanics, the Catholic church in the country would be in a sorry state. A full 18 million of the country's 65 million Roman Catholics are Latino, accounting for more than two-thirds of the new Catholics in the country since 1960.

Benedict's argument to these Catholics is multi-faceted. He insists that the obedience and discipline of the church is not constraining, but liberating. What the church offers, he insisted, is the freedom from the shackles of consumerism and relativism, which the pontiff sees as the two-headed beast of modernity. The Earth, he told an audience of 25,000 youths, "groans under the weight of consumerist greed and irresponsible exploitation."

Benedict may not be the "Rottweiler" critics pegged him, but he does not back down: "Is it consistent for practicing Catholics to ignore or exploit the poor and the marginalized, to promote sexual behavior contrary to Catholic moral teachings, or to adopt positions that contradict the right to life of every human being from conception to natural death?" he asked Catholic bishops. "Any tendency to treat religion as a private matter must be resisted."

That's a tough sell in a country whose wrestling match over religion's proper role in public life remains indecisive and volatile. But, for Benedict, faith is not an accessory, but the engine of life. "'Authority.' 'Obedience.' To be frank, these are not easy words to speak nowadays. Words like these represent a 'stumbling stone' for many of our contemporaries, especially in a society which rightly places a high value on personal freedom," the Pope said at Yankee Stadium. These were the remarks most media seized on, but their real meaning is in what followed:

"The Gospel teaches us that true freedom, the freedom of the children of God, is found only in the self-surrender which is part of the mystery of love. Only by losing ourselves, the Lord tells us, do we truly find ourselves. True freedom blossoms when we turn away from the burden of sin, which clouds our perceptions and weakens our resolve, and find the source of our ultimate happiness in him who is infinite love, infinite freedom, infinite life. 'In his will is our peace.'"

What Benedict is trying to say is that what complicates life is materialistic marginalia -- all those i Pods, Blackberries, cell phones, laptops, satellite dishes and DVRs to program, to break, to attend to. Much of the dis-ease that Americans feel comes from the manacles these goodies inflict.

Savonarola, too, was a critic of the excess and vanity of his age. Among his mistakes was a predilection for extremism. It won't take a zealot to inject life in the Catholic Church. Perhaps what the church most needs is a shepherd to try, as Benedict said, to "bind up the wounds" and remind us that what looks like liberty can be a lifetime of imprisonment.

LOSS: A TRILOGY

-1-

People May Be Broken But Never A Friendship

My friend has breast cancer.

It is Stage Four. There is no Stage Five. She tells me this in a telephone conversation from her home in Philadelphia. At the news, I begin to tremble, but hope she cannot hear it in my voice. In her voice, there is the sense of breaking it to me gently, the medical phrases parsed in a soothing, hopeful pitch.

But I know what I am dealing with. And so does she. We are smart women, Judi and I, *au courant* with all things cultural, political, and medical. We are news people, pointed, direct, arch and always cynical. This is not good news and we both know it.

It has been years since I have seen Judi and yet she is embedded in me the way kindred spirits can be. They are the ones offering parenthetical commentary to the running monologue in your head. They are the ones whose sardonic (and untranslatable) quips come to you in your most sour, down-on-the-world moments. They pick you up when they are not even there, phantoms that impress themselves on your soul with a tender, if occasionally unwelcome, gibe.

It is perhaps because you hear them in your head, and read them on the page and smirk at them in the street that you believe you are physically closer than you really are. Kindred spirits are omnipresent. Geography is merely a discomfiting reminder that the worlds of the mind and of the flesh are lamentably distant.

Judi and I have known each other nearly 20 years and were forged by fire, working together at a newspaper poisoned by economic downturn, patching together our jobs, and our lives, with mettle, sarcasm and pluck.

My life was slipping away from me then, as it does daily when you are in your 20s. In contrast, Judi's seemed to possess an aggravating serenity. That would have been enough for me to despise her had she not glinted with self-deprecating charm.

One Friday evening, as the newsroom was emptying out of people returning home to what I, in my fervid imagination, believed were the romantic embraces denied me, I collapsed in paroxysms of self-pity. Judi was there to invite me home for meatloaf. "Just think," she said, handing me a tissue and shaking me by the shoulders, "This will make great material for a novel one day."

I didn't know whether to hug her or hit her, a reaction to Judi's queer observations that would become common.

"You know how I feel about life, Trace…" she once told me. "We only get this one shot."

"Isn't that depressing?" I said.

"On the contrary," she said. "It's a triumph. Because we only get one chance to get it right. It gives life a kind of energy, you know, charges it with significance."

Time collapses when someone you love has cancer. It becomes denser, prismatic. Perhaps that is because everything else in your life, those desultory chores whose erratic tempo supplies so much of life's drama, take their proper place as trivia. Silhouetted against issues of life and death, love and loss, the measure of our days becomes part of the ephemera of distraction.

When your friend has cancer, you do not absent yourself from life. You show up for work. You nibble carrot sticks at parties. You go to the movies.

Because you are not related by genetics, you are not permitted the luxury of anguish. So you stifle it. You think you are unduly empathetic because all day long, and during the autumn nights that turn too swiftly to dark, you think of your friend and her rugged battle through a landscape you do not share.

In late summer, just before her transfiguring surgery, I walked with Judi through Rittenhouse Square in Philadelphia. Her bald head shielded by a bandanna, Judi told me how she walks to the park daily, sits on a bench and watches the motley stream of humanity stewing in the park.

There are the old women who dress exclusively in white and talk only to themselves -- and the squirrels. There are the young men in swollen jeans dancing to a metallic hum streaming into their ears.

There are the young women who nuzzle their babies to their lips and whisper stories for dreaming. "And you know," Judi said, "I look around and I realize, we're all broken."

And I can only chuckle, because the observation is pure Judi, this acidic alloy of wryness and compassion.

Because we are kindred spirits, I need no translation. We are all chipped and mottled, she is saying, glued together and torn asunder, all of us needing time at the body shop, the beauty parlor, or maybe the shrink.

So that later, driving over the Ben Franklin Bridge with Philadelphia receding in the rear-view mirror, I turn the phrase over in my mind and wonder how I have gone so long without Judi at my elbow to offer snippets of sardonic insight. Being apart seems not only impossible, but indecent. How could I have let this happen?

I have worn out my welcome at the post office. I have sent cards and books and flowers and cookies. I try to send myself in every little package, but I don't seem to fit. After a while, it is hard to fashion a new line for the "Get well" card, so hackneyed do the solicitous phrases become. After a while, all you want to say is, "You are suffering. And I am not there. And that is not right."

-2-

When Frankness Is The Hardest Gift

The cancer has spread. My friend Judi, who has Stage 4 breast cancer, informs me of the disease's progression from her home in Philadelphia. She is breathless and weary. There is a catch in her throat, a hint of the inroads the disease has made in her lungs. For the last few weeks she has had a cough. An irritating but persistent annoyance that finally led her back into her doctor's office for a CAT scan, which revealed the latest insidious development.

"It's not good," Judi says, and my heart sinks. I fumble for words, terrified and conscious of not revealing my terror.

"What does that mean?" I say, searching for specifics.

"It means it spread faster than I thought it would," she says.

The cancer has evaded every blistering barrage of science and wormed its way into my friend's vital organ, where it festers.

We are back to square one.

Or maybe we are moving backward.

In the dizzying contest between cancer and man, it is difficult to know for sure.

For the last 10 months, Judi has waged a battle with breast cancer with a barrage of toxins, surgery and radiation. In my mind, I see the toxins dripping into her veins and imagine them bleaching out the poison and making my friend whole again. Already, she has lost both breasts and much of her hair. The hair, I can see from a photograph, has grown in. It is short and curly and makes her look like Judi Dench.

Three months ago, she was fired from her job, as the spokesman for the Maryland Port Administration. In a few months, she will have no health insurance.

The firing was an insult, but it wasn't fatal. It was a violation that made her indignant and vulnerable. But to fight it -- or even to brood about it -- took too much energy. When you have cancer, you learn to ration that energy. But here's the cruel reality about fighting cancer: You do not get a reprieve from the rest of your life. It goes on with callous insistence, indifferent to your capacity to respond.

Another cruel reality: The notion of "fighting" cancer itself is something of a ruse. Most of the time you do not fight. Most of the time you wait. You wait to see how -- or if -- the drugs work. You wait for the next treatment. You wait for test results. You wait for doctors to confer. You wait for them to explain your options to you.

And while you wait, the cancer grows.

Or maybe it does not. Maybe it lies dormant, patient as a scorpion. The problem is, you do not know. You exist most of the time in this emotional limbo, not sure whether you are winning or losing a battle whose playing field you can never see.

"I guess they'll suggest more chemo," I say, hopefully.

"Probably," says Judi. And then she says, hesitantly, "and then I'll have a decision to make."

"What does that mean?"

"Well, there's the quality of life issue," she says. "Do I really want to poison myself again? Do I really want to go through all of that?"

I grow quiet. I want to say, "What do you mean, quality of life? What do you mean, a choice? Isn't there only one choice, to rage, rage, against the dying of the light?" But I say nothing, not only because it is impudent, but because of an impending sorrow I cannot shake.

I remember an interview with Dr. Sherwin Nuland, author of the best seller *How We Die*. We were discussing end-of-life decisions and what Nuland clearly considered the charade of "death with dignity." There is no dignity with death, he told me.

Taking me by surprise, he told me he was against euthanasia because he said, "You do not belong only to yourself. You belong to a community of people."

When Judi broached the inevitable subject of treatment, I understood Nuland's perspective with greater clarity. And I understood, too, the shred of selfishness in friendships. We have friends largely for their buoying effect on our own moods. We keep those who are captivating and uplifting and discard those who are draining or hurtful. But, too, there is what we give them, the stories we impart, the concerns, misgivings and insights that give our friends a privileged insight into who we are. The selfishness is rooted in the singularity of that insight.

Because nobody knows you as well as your very intimate friends, more is at stake in their existence. When they go, a part of you goes with them.

Judi and I have a mutual friend who, on hearing the news said she actually felt sorry for the world to lose someone as captivating as Judi. I told her I was more selfish than that. I told her that I couldn't muster that degree of altruism when one of the few people who knew so much about me -- and liked me just the same, imagine! -- might not be there to share my son's high school graduation.

In the ensuing days and months of dreadful treatment and dire decisions I suspect I will have to learn to sacrifice the part of friendship that is stingy for itself. I will have to learn to understand my friend's will and bury my own.

That is the only dignity left in this grim ordeal.

-3-

Rushing To Sit By The Side Of An Angel

Walk toward the angel, the woman said. I thought: *You must be kidding.*

Philadelphia's 30th Street train station greets visitors with an enormous bronze sculpture of a muscular angel, holding a limp, lifeless male figure in its certain, steady grasp. The look on the angel's face is resolute and serene. It was nothing like mine.

I had rushed to Philadelphia from New Haven to be by the side of my dearest friend, Judi, who was dying of breast cancer. She had wanted me to come, called me, spoke to me in a voice so sluggish and numb I scarcely recognized it. "I want you to know," she said, "that you are welcome."

And I packed my bag.

Judi had steadfastly resisted my earlier entreaties to visit. Part of it was her nature. She hadn't much strength. She wasn't, she said, "the queen of the hop." I didn't care. But she did. Much of her resistance had to do with the nature of our relationship. Judi was 17 years older than I. There was always a maternal element to her affection for me. She loved me too much to let me know how sick she was. She thought it would devastate me. In that, as in so many things, she was right.

To rush to the side of a dying friend isn't an experience most of us get, and most of us are grateful for this, a gratitude I soon learned was foolish. We think we know what love is. But most of us never even come close. Most of us skitter around the edges, drawn more by affection than love. I'm as guilty and selfish as most, maybe more. On the train, I shook with apprehension. What if I collapsed at the sight of her? What if

I cried? What if I didn't make it in time? What if Judi could sense my anguish?

"We both know I have this thing," Judi had written me weeks before. "We both knew the odds." Oh, yes, Judi, but we both know what an Irish sentimentalist I am. We both knew that my hope would eclipse my reason. All of the packages, all of the cards, all of the teddy bears and pajama tops and audio books and soda bread I sent all attested to the sheer, physical force of my will. My faith. My belief in miracles.

Angels. We look for them everywhere. On our shoulders. In the heavens. On teddy bears and wallpaper and bumper stickers. But standing under that imposing angel in Philadelphia's train station, I thought: What happens when the angel is you?

I could no longer hope for an angel's blessing. I was the angel. Unworthy. Unskilled. Ill-equipped, doubtful and needy. All of the candles I lit, the prayers I offered, the novenas that asked for God's mercy and grace suddenly rebounded on me with a realization so stunning it was like an assault. Maybe God doesn't intervene with dramatic pyrotechnics. Maybe intervention is that soulful jolt we get when we realize that what we are here for is to be angels for one another.

As Judi would say, that's what you get when you ask for Free Will.

Judi. Always quick with the derisive quip. She could defuse a situation with a witty denial that was (take your pick) grossly off-color or desperately welcome. In one of her last e-mails to me in which she downplayed the appearance of the maddeningly aggressive lumps that appeared on her long, slender neck, she confided, unusually and uneasily for Judi, that she wondered about her own stamina to keep going. After all, she wrote, "I'm the one who quit field hockey in the 7th grade as soon as I got a cramp in my side. Also the one who prayed for death when I got a 'C' on a paper freshman year in college. Considered flushing myself down the toilet in the ladies room in the library. Settled for flushing the essay down. Oy."

In retrospect I think she was trying to tell me she couldn't do it anymore, an acknowledgment all too evident when I saw her, sallow and emaciated in her hospital bed in Philadelphia. Heavily sedated, afflicted with interminable bouts of nausea, she greeted me with a warm, but effortful smile. I held her hand. She managed a squeeze. "This is what the end looks like," she said. "Whaddya think?" She slept. I buried my head into her side. I would not weep, I told myself. I would not. But tears dripped onto the hospital sheets, through the bedding, onto her thighs. For a moment, she woke. Her fingers, long, tapering and weak, combed my hair. "I know this is difficult for you," she said.

But it wasn't. Not really. In the hours I spent beside her, listening to the rattle in her respiration, the frightened, sudden intake of breath as she slept, I bathed her face in warm, perfumed cloths. When she vomited, I painted her dry lips with a swab of peppermint mouthwash. She inclined her head toward mine. The solace was palpable.

I thought I was supposed to be the angel. It was Judi all along.

Not long before she was so reduced, Judi wrote me in reaction to a column I had written on "The Passion," and my discomfort at seeing Jesus as a hapless victim. Judi, who was Jewish but had read all the gospels, wrote, "I don't think of Jesus as a victim -- I think that through it all he was at once in it and above it. He suffered but with the understanding of the limitations of what man can do to man. He understood the finite versus the infinite. This is a soothing recognition to anyone going through a horrendous situation -- pain might have you in its grips, but not forever. Whereas love of the divine sort doesn't dissipate."

My dear friend Judi Scioli, who was one of the most brilliant people I ever met, died three days after I left her. She had the grace to allow me to minister to her, a benediction that is her most enduring gift to me. She understood life in a way most of us can never hope to, with an intellect and compassion evidenced in one of her last e-mails to me.

She had, she said, forgotten all her Latin, her French and Italian. She no longer read Faulkner with breakfast or Joyce with dinner. Once she had taught transformational syntax, read Dante and Ovid in the original. "Now," she wrote, "I'm afraid that if I try to re-read Umberto Eco I will reveal myself as the total moron I have become."

"But today I can go into a waiting room where half a dozen people from all walks of life are waiting for their radiation treatments or chemo or whatever and not a single one of them seems like a stranger. Sometimes I know their names and sometimes I don't. Some I know where they come from and some I don't. But my head's not in either *People* magazine or Pirandello. I'm right there, in that room, and there really isn't very much anyone can tell me about the history of ideas or particle physics. Don't get me wrong -- I'm all for enlightenment with a capital 'E.' My hat is off to all the brilliant people working on great books and doing research and breaking codes. Some of them do wonderful things for mankind. But in the end, baby, people are as scared and vulnerable and brave as they were before they lit the first fire in a cave."

New Icon: A Frump For Society To Covet

Marge Simpson is on the cover of *Maxim* this month. *Maxim*, that mainstream pusher of cheesecake, has elevated Marge, the doyenne of D'oh-eyed domesticity, to the pantheon of buxom airheads that populate its misogynist fantasy.

Poor Marge.

Just look at her, rag in hand, buttocks in the air, knees spread suggestively, Dairy Queen bouffant tied up in a towel, breasts soaked with dirty water, "every man's ideal wife," say the sophomoric editors of *Maxim*, "curvy, wild haired, and willing to accept a fat, balding drunk loser as her knight in shining armor." And there you have it, ladies, the sex symbol of the modern age: a throaty, blue-haired doormat with retro hair and cheap jewelry who can be drawn to any specification you would like: Marge Simpson, the New Age Stepford wife.

Say what you will about Paris Hilton, Britney Spears and any number of vacuous blondes in tawdry thongs -- what a man really wants is a compliant lap dog willing to overlook his passion for burping contests and generic beer. A living doll to be manipulated however her Average Joe deems fit.

The Frump is hip.

And just in time, too. After all, how many episodes of "Average Joe," the reality series that dangles a comely young woman in front of portly, balding, periodontally-challenged middle-aged men and then dares her not to fall in love with them, do you have to watch before you start to ask: Where's "Average Jane?" Well there she is. She's on the cover of *Maxim*, mopping the floor.

Dowdy is the New Man's sultry.

So, at least, says *The New Yorker,* which should know something about dowdy. As evidence, it points to the designs of Prada, whose frowzy mélange of pleats and plaids connote what the magazine calls a "slightly frumpy, somewhat feminist... alternative aesthetic." *The Washington Post* noted that Prada's "womanly aesthetic" alternates between an "offbeat austerity to frumpy intellectualism."

There's that word again.

It's not, perhaps, a coincidence that Prada's offbeat fashion has caught on with an increasingly intellectualized population of women. The number of women earning Ph.Ds has increased by more than 50 percent in the last 10 years, growing at more than twice the rate of the number of men getting those degrees. About 40 percent of women 45 to 54 years old are employed in a managerial or professional occupation, reports American Demographics. These women spend a whopping $23.3 billion on clothes, or more than twice what teenagers spend.

These women don't have time for stiletto heels and Wonder bras. They're lucky if they can get their stockings on without running. No wonder opaque is in. And they're often on their feet all day, which has done wonders for Birkenstock.

Marge may not have the credentials these women have, but she's in an age bracket that's becoming increasingly tantalizing for advertisers. After years of turning a cold shoulder to older women as if they were a bunch of coupon-cutting fusspots pining for Lawrence Welk reruns, advertisers are discovering that Marge and her ilk have lots of dough and time to spend it.

The Wall Street Journal reports that after years of appealing to erratic twentysomethings, "some of the world's best-known companies are setting their sights on older consumers, an audience habitually written off as poor, excessively frugal or stuck in a rut of buying the same brand."

What got Madison Avenue to wake up and take notice, the *Journal* reports, was Ted Koppel's reaction when ABC was threatening to deep-six Koppel's "Nightline" program because it skewed heavily toward older viewers. Koppel offered this revelatory retort: "Sixty- and 70-year-old people buy things," he said.

D'oh!

And they don't want terrycloth housecoats. *The New York Times* reports that women's clothiers have made the startling discovery that older women need clothes.

More astonishingly, they'd like something a little more jaunty than a caftan. The *Times* quotes unnamed merchants asserting that baby boomers "may not have the figures they did in college, but they still want up-to-date fashion, including sprightly flowered dresses and embroidered jackets."

What do you know? A sprightly flowered dress on a 45-year-old. Now all she needs to do is tie her hair up into a snow cone, grab a toilet brush and hope she's spotted by a *Maxim* photographer looking for a new centerfold.

Soft Scrub, anyone?

Stalking The Predator Within

Even now, I find it difficult to call him a predator.

Perhaps it's because I'm not sure where that label leaves me.

I've read that victims tend to be hesitant to condemn their oppressors. No doubt, there's some sort of psychoanalytical matrix to that. But the most chilling, and enduring memories are the ambiguous ones, the ones that were and weren't what you thought, the ones without resolution, the ones that still leave you a little queasy even though it's undeniable that you survived, after all.

I met Mr. Willson when I was 18 years old, home alone after my first year in college, and irrevocably lonely. My mother was working in Provincetown for the summer and I was charged with caring for my 12-year-old brother who, even then, had a more interesting life than I. Most of my time was spent alone under a self-imposed monastic discipline. I read. I ran. I sat, pointlessly, in the sun on a beige bridge chair, slathered in baby oil, desperate for the elusive suburban tan.

On Sundays, I walked to Mass and was typically picked up by a neighbor, who pulled to the side of the road and told me to "hop in." It was that kind of a time. It was that kind of a place.

Mr. Willson was one of these neighbors. He drove a tomato red Ford truck with a battered white camper snapped to the cab. Every afternoon, around 4, he drove it slowly past my house, the driver's window down and his left elbow propped along the window jam. I used to see him on my daily run. He began by simply waving at me. Not a wave, but a kind of salute of recognition. I waved back.

One afternoon, just as I was sprinting the last 50 yards home, Mr. Willson's truck pulled up beside me. He sat in the car as I jogged up and said it was becoming rather awkward to wave to someone to whom he had not formally introduced himself. "I'm Tom Willson," he said. "Two Ls, and that's an L of a difference."

Our acquaintance began.

I would not say Mr. Willson, a 64-year-old retiree, managed to drive by every day just as I was sprinting home, but it was close. He would sit in the cab of his truck and ask me questions about myself -- my college career, my work aspirations, what I liked to read. From there, he offered copious practical, almost paternal advice on a regular basis: Where I should invest my money. What type of car I should own. How I should always carry 3-inch-by-5-inch index cards for stray thoughts and abrupt measuring assignments. "Every blue line is one-quarter of an inch," he offered helpfully. "Comes in handy."

He spoke with a courtly civility that was so painstakingly gracious it was almost quaint. He mentioned other families in the neighborhood I knew well. Knowing I was interested in journalism and France, he would drop by with newspapers -- the *Ottawa Citizen* was a favorite -- and topical maps of Normandy from his days in the Army.

I cannot say that all of his contributions were appreciated, but their thoughtfulness made me grateful -- and suspicious. I fretted over his attentions even as I was charmed by them. I was not then aware of the expression, *quid pro quo*, but surely I understood the exchange.

But the truth was that no one else had paid me such dedicated attention. No one else, creepily, had been as actively interested.

Not long after the priest pedophilia scandal in the Archdiocese of Boston, I spoke with an expert in pedophilia who told me how perpetrators target kids. "One man (I treated) told me, 'I can look around a school yard and tell you who is an easy mark,'" Nicholas Groth, a clinical psychologist and former director of the sex offender program at the Connecticut Correctional Institution at Somers, told me. "It's the child who is alone. It's the child who no one is paying any attention to. Maybe it's cold out and it's the child with the thin coat who isn't dressed warmly."

Late that summer, Mr. Willson asked me to dinner. Actually, he had been asking me for some time. He did so with the pragmatic grace I had come to expect. I would be picked up by 6. I would return by 8. The menu was Italian. There were early-bird specials. After several clumsy refusals, I conceded.

It did not take long, sitting in the garishly overdone dining room, the walls decorated with campy Venetian gondolas and Jerry Vale crooning from the speakers, that I began to feel sick. Perhaps it was his stiff but earnest admission of how much the evening meant to him. Perhaps it was his staring at me with livery brown eyes. Or perhaps I was sick with my own knowledge of the inevitability of his affections. But I suddenly realized the severity of my plight.

Mr. Willson brought me home, as promised, before 8. He wanted me to come by sometime, he said, to retrieve a gift he had for me. I promised I would but never had my front door looked so good -- and so remote. As I placed my hand on the door handle, he leaned over. He moved to kiss me. I turned my cheek, snapped the door open and tumbled out. "I'm sorry," he said. He blushed. "I should never have presumed...."

But I no longer heard him. I turned on my heels and rushed toward the door and double locked it behind me. How could I have been so stupid?

A few years ago, I returned to my hometown and cycled past what had been Mr. Willson's house. It's been razed, like so many homes in my neighborhood, and replaced by a Mc Mansion. Mr. Willson died six years ago. I read his obituary in the paper and the news filled me with more than a little pity. Even now, I find his loneliness pathetic. Even now, I wonder if I misjudged him.

Mr. Wilson never lived to see the Internet. If he had, I feel certain it would have expanded his base of targets substantially. The world is full of lost and lonely children. It is amazing how much a little attention can assuage.

Best Friends Forever, Or Maybe Not

The day after Christmas, my son's best friend came over to examine the loot.

On a frosty, languid day, the snow gone Styrofoam stiff and the sky a frigid, steely blue, PJ and his best buddy tore through the Wheat Thins and Goldfish, the Jolly Rancher Fruit Chews and Hershey's Kisses, running sock-less through the house, sliding madly on the waxed floors.

"Pretend, pretend, this car is an eyeball car and he's coming toward you," says PJ.

"No, no, pretend, pretend this bear is riding the helicopter," says his friend.

"And pretend he's being chased by this gorilla."

"And the gorilla's got a seeing eyeball."

"And pretend..."

And on it goes, in this marvelous, frenetic syncopation that is part imagination and part glee. This strange collage of conversation, in which one starts a fiction and the other embellishes it, is magical to me, like music. I had forgotten how easy and entrancing it could be to create a world out of whole cloth, where animals talk and fly and drive cars, and where cars scamper up vines and swim through icy currents. "Pretend, pretend, pretend," they say, in a boyish metronome that always finds an object.

PJ and his pal, whom I'll call Michael, have been best friends since infancy, an affection borne of convenience and necessity. My husband and I were friendly with Michael's parents, and so we swapped the boys, beginning when they were in their bassinets and continuing until...when?

"Michael, Michael, Michael," PJ squeals, jumping up and down on the sofa as if it were a trampoline. "Let's play together every day the day after Christmas until we're old!"

PJ is holding a stuffed yellow dog by its neck and skipping merrily through the den.

He is 6 years old now and I wonder what "old" means to him. I am sitting at the kitchen table, lingering over the Christmas cards we received, noting who keeps up the tradition and who has fallen off. It occurs to me, as PJ and Michael race their Hot Wheels through the den, that I don't have a single card from someone I knew when I was 6. I don't think I sent one, either. All of those people -- the toddlers to whom I promised eternal affection, the classmates with whom I exchanged dishy secrets, teenagers with whom I shared stories of clumsy love -- have all faded into the vapor of my past.

It isn't as if my professed fidelity was false. I fully intended to cling to these objects of my affection until my last breath.

But, of course, I didn't.

I often hear stories about friends who were in nursery school together, or who lost their first teeth on the same day, or discarded their training wheels in the same week. These people are still friends and have an enviably rich skein of history that connects them. But what on earth is there that magnetizes us at 6? Could it still be there at 60? Or is it gnarled, scuffed by time, circumstance and the inconsistency of our own hearts?

When I was 6 years old, I had a best friend called Judy who merited the position solely due to her affection for Bazooka bubble gum and Captain America comics. At 12, my best friend was a tall, lanky espresso-colored girl named Laura, with whom I discussed Watergate, the Chevrolet Vega and "The Bionic Woman." I lost Laura when a group of African-American students beat her up over acting "too white," and she fled to a private school.

At 16, my best friend was Julie, a fellow athlete and A-student whom I was forever pulling out of the mire of adolescent angst.

In our yearbooks, we pledged lifelong fidelity and wept openly as we threw our mortarboards into the air.

Within seven years, both Julie and I would lose our husbands -- mine to desertion, hers to death. Our relationship foundered, too, on my clumsy and caustic attempt to assuage her grief. The loss of our friendship haunts me, but my fevered attempts to suture it back to what it was were futile. Some wounds are too deep to tend.

"I love Michael because he always gives me a break," PJ volunteers one evening, as we walk the dog.

I try to process this in the January twilight. Part of me wonders if boys are more forgiving and less invasive than girls, who tend to insinuate and infer, mucking about in the miasma of emotion. But mostly I simply luxuriate in the innocent enormity of my son's affections. I look over at his buoyant steps and join him in the wonder of this first and best love, hoping, along with him, that it will last until he and his pal are very, very old.

My Father's Christmas Blues

My father always hated this time of year. Gave him the blues, he said. Christmas always made him think of the people he'd lost in his life, the aunts, the uncles, the cabal of Irish faces that clustered around his mother's shimmering aluminum Christmas tree. Every new Christmas seemed to leave him short one more family member, and give him one more reason for despair.

I never understood. Aren't we enough? I would think. Didn't one's own children, red-cheeked and animated, restore whatever -- or whoever -- was lost?

No. They do not.

On June 2, after riding his bike through the puddles of a late afternoon shower, my father, Barry T. O'Shaughnessy, 62, collapsed and died of a massive heart attack. He had been to his doctor only a day before, pronouncing himself in excellent health. There were no conditions, no signs. From what we could tell, he never felt anything more than a little punky. He died at the top of the street where we grew up, the place he had hoped to find all his happiness.

Only days before, I had written a column about the announced closing of his childhood church, outside of Boston. He would not live to see the column published. On the day it was printed, we attended his funeral Mass in that same church, the place from which, three years before, we had buried my grandmother, and three years before that, my uncle. We had lost them all in six years.

I take my son along the broad avenues of the street where my father grew up, the Brigham's ice cream shop on the corner where my father bought us dollops of butternut ice cream served in chilly pewter vases. We buy our pizza at Nicola's, where my grandmother and uncle always bought a large cheese after Saturday Mass. Our cold cuts we buy at D'Agostino's, where my father bought my grandmother hot meals wrapped in cellophane that he served her on a linoleum TV tray. All of these places, these streets, are freighted with memory for me, memory to which my own son has no access.

My father understood that. Death erases and erodes. The unspoken codes, the unconscious rhythms, the peculiar reflexes that you share with the dead evaporate with their passing. And you long for them as deeply as you do the familiar scent of Palmolive soap and Barbasol that attends their memory.

On the Christmas Eve nights when my father sat beneath the innocuous painting of a babbling brook, his feet on the embroidered ottoman, I saw the shadow of loss cross his face. It was not that he couldn't recall the Christmases of his youth, when his mother would set up the tree, slather the living room in garland and wrap the presents -- all in one night. He could recall them. But he couldn't bring them back.

What he missed is what I miss: the three-dimensionality of memory. I miss not the flamboyant moments, but the mundane ones. I miss the insignificant details of his life that, stirred together, created the richness of him. The jaunty, musical way his foot danced in the air as he slurped maple walnut ice cream at Bedford Farms. The yeasty regularity of his life, in which each oil change, each mile cycled, each appliance purchased was meticulously logged in a black spiral notebook, receipts carefully annotated by date. How do I explain to my son what it was like to watch my father leaning sweatily over a sink, the curl of his widow's peak dangling over his crimson brow, scrutinizing my bike tube for the bubbles that would indicate a puncture. "I got him," he'd say, spotting the incriminating gurgle. My father had solved another catastrophe.

How do I explain what I felt, spotting my father in the third pew at St. James, arms folded across his little belly, thick bottom lip protruding, glancing toward the doors of the church, looking for me. And the broad smile when I came and sat beside him, the arm across my shoulder, the missal placed gently in my hand. "How are you?" he'd say in his broad Boston accent. "When did you get in?"

Perhaps because my time with my father was so constrained, it became more precious. My parents' marriage collapsed in 1970, when divorce was still such an anomaly that I can still remember my histrionic uncle running around the house, whispering frantically, "Don't tell the relatives in Ireland!"

And yet my father saw us faithfully, every single weekend, dividing himself into kaleidoscopic parts to satisfy his own three children and the three step-children he acquired when he remarried in 1974.

On Saturday afternoons, when the weather was fair, he'd take all six of us down to Pierce School, wielding a wooden bat and a flimsy baseball glove. "It's a high, fly ball," he'd say in his best falsetto, watching the ball arc through the clear blue sky. "One hand for show-offs," he'd warn us. "Two hands for baseball players." My father was unimpressed by flamboyance, preferring instead a dutiful caution that bordered on mania.

This hardly prevented him from playing the fool. On the basketball court, where we'd play "PIG" and "HORSE," my father would strain for gymnastic and burlesque shots. "Six against one!" he'd cry, taking on the ragged assembly of children who longed to hear his affirming "What a shot!"

I used to bike with my father on a broad paved path that took the place of the old Boston and Maine railway tracks. The bikes were so much sleeker than the rickety old Sears he taught me to ride when I was 5. "Watch me," he'd say, straddling his own enormous Ross, pedals reflecting the afternoon light. "Wait up," I'd say, pedals whirring madly, training wheels squealing gratingly. Eventually, I caught up, or he slowed down.

And we'd pedal on together to the dirt road where the ice cream truck stopped every evening. A Creamsicle shared with my father stopped the world.

That is my image of him now: Flying down the bike path, odometer flickering, wheels whirring, windbreaker lifting in the breeze. On that path, where he managed to be both man and child, I see him as a boy again, rushing home to his mother and brother, young and incandescent knowing he was headed home, to the embrace of his family. Home, home, to that place where "peace comes dropping slow."

Wait for me, Dad. Wait for me.

What A Father Kept Safe

The *Globe* box was a small, wood cigar box my father kept in his office at *The Boston Globe*, where he worked for 41 years. After he retired, his *Globe* box went with him -- not to his home, but to a sooty dimple in my grandmother's cellar, where my father kept all his private effects. There, nobody would rummage through the mementos my father held most intimate, and most dear.

The *Globe* box was full of me.

Or, more precisely, the thoughts, words, musings and commentary I had sent my father, addressed to his office at the *Globe*, for more than 25 years. Until I held it, in the shadow of my grandmother's looming Victorian home, I never knew it existed.

Now I am a letter sender, a spasmodic and compulsive sender of letters, clippings, cards and packages. Over the years, I imagine I sent hundreds of notes and missives to my father, some pedestrian and some poignant. Had he kept every scrap of doggerel and fancy I sent his way, he would have required a storage locker. Instead, there was merely this cigar box, compact and quaint, that held only the most essential words, those with which he could not part.

Four years earlier, my father and I had sliced through the honeycomb of my grandmother's home. The two of us were clearing out her hauntingly empty home in the days and weeks after her death. My grandmother was a scrappy, frugal woman, and there was little in her house of great material worth.

Her jewelry, what there was of it, was costume. Her clothes, polyester. Her furniture, particle board. She neither spent much on herself nor indulged anyone to spend much on her. And so looking around at this accretion, my father shook his head in resignation.

"You work and sacrifice your whole life, and what does it all add up to?" he sighed. "A heap of junk."

And yet out of those warrens of inferior materials and obsolete appliances, I longed to pluck some jewel. There must be some essence of my grandmother that could be distilled into one, precious, emblematic thing. Something to hold on to. Something to prize. But there was nothing. And in the hours and weeks after my father's sudden death, I sought the same physical manifestation of my father, and felt again the hungry pang of heartache at the recognition that my desire was elusive.

And then, the box.

All of us are recipients of some gift or letter or memento. Americans send 7 billion greeting cards alone in a year. Most of them will be discarded, I suppose, in the way most of the gifts we receive this holiday will blend and blur into our possessions, ultimately breaking or burdening, going out of fashion or out of use. But what is it that we keep of these offerings? And what do those things say, not just about the giver, but the recipient?

In fits of temper, or disappointment, I have burned the journals of my youth, or the blind professions of love from some discarded suitor. I threw every book, letter and postal card from one such lover down an apartment incinerator after the relationship imploded. It felt cathartic at the time, but I have had spasms of regret over it. But there are things that I cannot part with, things as patently cherished as a lock of my son's hair, and as ugly and useless as the penguin Christmas ornament my husband bought me at a 7-11 in the winter of 1989.

My father kept cards in which I expressed my devotion and appears to have discarded those in which I unleashed my anguish. He kept one column, a little piece I wrote years ago, of a summer when I was 5, and he taught me how to ride a bike. "I think I can, I think I can," he shouted encouragingly, as I wobbled fitfully away.

It was an image he had half-forgotten until I laid it all down for him, and, once remembered, kept with him always. But why this column? And why that postcard? And why this flimsy, torn ticket stub to "Chariots of Fire?" And what of the rest of the letters? Where are they?

What I have of my father is not what he gave me -- but what he kept of me. And what he kept spoke of what he could not say. But now it whispers to me, in those hours of isolation when his loss is the most deep. Then I join him in the memory of summer, pedaling spastically on my two-wheeler, veiled in his embrace, hoping he would never let go, knowing he must, eager to show him how well I could stay afloat without him.

My Son Has Developed
An Irrational Fear Of Bees

My son has developed an irrational fear of bees. Hyacinths bloom along the foundation of the house, bringing with them the menacing buzz of insects, many of them bees and all of them, in my son's overactive imagination, out to get him.

He will not go outside.

This is ridiculous, I tell him. "You are the last thing on a bee's mind," I tell him, but he reminds me that I have no access to the mind of a bee, nor any particular aptitude for deciphering it, and so we are back to the absurdity of unreasonable fear.

This anxiety is of long incubation. Last summer, during Vacation Bible School, my son was stung by a bee for the first time in his life. Evidently, the event sufficiently traumatized him to develop into a full-fledged phobia and has probably ruined my chances for Vacation Bible School this summer to boot.

Scientists say that bad memories are particularly more tenacious than good ones for evolutionary reasons; the adrenaline involved in frightening experiences appears to seal in emotionally charged memories. Dr. Larry Cahill, a professor Neurobiology and Behavior at the University of California-Irvine, found that emotional arousal helps us remember threatening events and circumstances -- like my son's bee sting.

So, my mother was right; we do remember bad events better than good ones, largely because benign memories don't pose a threat and are, from the evolutionary standpoint, worthless.

My son falsely believes that I can defend him from the bees, a degree of faith I hardly merit. But the problem is that all children believe their parents can shield them from peril, a delusion largely of our own making. "I'm here," we whisper. "You're safe."

In the stage adaptation of Joan Didion's *The Year of Magical Thinking*, now playing at TheaterWorks in Hartford, Didion wonders about the deception inherent in maternal reassurance. "Did I lie to you?" she asks her fatally ill daughter, Quintana. "Did I lie to you all my life? When I said, 'You're safe, I'm here,' was that a lie or did you believe it? Is a lie only a story that the hearer disbelieves? Is that the only definition of a life? Or did you believe it?"

When I was 25 and living outside Washington, D.C., I became chronically ill with mononucleosis, I had trouble breathing. I couldn't move without pain. I dreamed in sweaty, tempestuous whorls of color. I was unable to work.

"You'll be fine," my mother told me initially, convinced it was merely a virus. "You're as healthy as a horse." After six months with no improvement, my mother phoned me and, receiving the same bleak report, broke down in tears. "I can't do anything for you!" she wailed. "When you were young and you fell, I could stop the bleeding and hold you in my arms and make it better, but I can't do that now."

That was the moment when I discovered that my mother was powerless against fate, a shattering epiphany that baptized me into adulthood. We had both lost -- she her magical curative powers and I, my ability to believe in them.

When my son asks me to hold him as we pad through the garden, I feel empowered by the fervor of his trust, and complicit in this vital deception of childhood. Soon, sooner than I wish, I will no more be able to protect him from bees as I can from failed friendships, unrequited love of the indiscriminate ailments of mind and spirit. So much of tragedy is mercilessly bee-like, arbitrary and excruciating. The only way to steel oneself for it is by a little magical thinking, believing for a brief, evanescent while, that mommy can protect us from everything.

The Only Constant Is Change --
Even In Religion

For as long as I could remember, my grandmother and uncle went to Mass together.

On Saturday evenings, they brought me along, enfolding me into their filial relationship with all its strange rituals and intractable traditions. At St. Camilla's Church, in the fourth pew from the front, my uncle would lace the toe of his shoe against the kneeler and help my grandmother get to her knees to pray. As her eyesight deteriorated, he would thumb through her chocolate brown St. Joseph's Missal, finding the appropriate page, which he pointed to with his slender, bitten-to-pieces fingers. At the offertory, he opened his Buxton tri-fold wallet and handed her a dollar bill.

Once, during the exchange of peace, an old woman in a hat shook my uncle's hand with tears in her eyes. "There is a special place in heaven," she said, "for a son who treats his dear mother like that."

These days, my son and I are the only Catholics in the house. On Saturday nights, I grab him, a knapsack full of crayons and books, and head off to Mass. If he behaves, I tell my son, I'll get him a Happy Meal.

At Mass, PJ sits and tries to find Waldo, or traces the outlines of a maze with a burnt sienna crayon. I have managed to get him to stand for the Our Father, and shake hands with the strangers around him during the exchange of peace. I do not think PJ likes Mass, but he goes, perhaps to earn himself a Happy Meal, or to visit the goldfish in the meditation pond behind the church, or because, as a 6-year-old, he has no choice.

I think about my grandmother and uncle during these times, and wonder whether, 30 years from now, PJ will steady my elbow as I reach for Communion, or hand me a $5 bill for the offertory.

I wonder if he will be beside me at all. I wonder, alas, if he will even still be Catholic.

Last week, the Pew Forum on Religion & Public Life reported that nearly half of American adults have left the faith tradition of their childhood to either switch allegiances or abandon religious affiliation altogether.

Although the majority of Americans -- 78 percent -- still identify as Christian, only 51 percent of us are Protestant, and that number is slipping. One in four young (18 to 29) adults claim no religious affiliation.

The religion that has suffered the most from religious ambivalence or abhorrence is Roman Catholicism. My church has lost more members than any faith tradition from affiliation, the survey reports. Almost one in three Americans were raised Catholic but fewer than one in four have remained Catholic. Among Protestants, the story is similar. Mainline Protestant denominations like Methodists and Episcopal are losing out to nondenominational Protestant churches, mostly evangelical.

"The trend is towards more personal religion, and evangelicals offer that," Stephen Prothero, chairman of the religion department at Boston University, told *The New York Times*. "Those losing out are offering impersonal religion, and those winning are offering a smaller scale."

Scholars say the biggest revelation in the Pew study is the fluidity in religious affiliation. As Pew Forum director Luis Lugo told Time magazine, religion is just one in a slew of choices Americans make, where loyalty is far from job No. 1.

Americans, he said, "not only change jobs, change where they live, and change spouses, but they change religions, too."

That's interesting because, as Prothero and Boston College's Alan Wolfe have repeatedly written, American religion is more homogeneous than it ever was. The difference between a Methodist and a Lutheran is lost on most Americans, most of whom cannot even name the four Gospels. As Wolfe told PBS, "The notion that there are specific ideas associated with specific religions [has] been lost in American culture."

So why bother shifting from one squishy religion about which you know very little, to the next?

It's tempting to say that all this shifting bespeaks a kind of moral ambivalence, a kind of spiritual flaccidity. Americans, awash in a torrent of choice, can hardly be blamed for exercising their media-given right to caprice. Resolution, to a country intoxicated by change, can seem ornery, mulish, or just plain quaint.

I have often been critical about people who make life-changing decisions about religion based on what amounts to a fourth-grade education. Too much of church dis-affiliation comes from individuals whose only investment in their religion is to put their duff in a pew. Some of the "churn" in religious denominations is from people who choose a religion as they would choose a sofa -- for comfort's sake.

But there is another side to this religious churn. People are searching for something deeper than themselves. Religious books are the most impressive growth category in book publishing. Two thousand years after Pontius Pilate, we're still asking "What is truth?"

I retain what may be a foolishly romantic hope that my son will always be near me in faith, as in life. But if I have done my job, the values my faith espouses will be ingrained in him, and better gird him to ask that question, wherever it may lead.

No, A Divorce Is Not Just The Two Of You

Last night, my brother told his son that he is getting a divorce. It was the conversation he had dodged and choked on, the inevitability he had hoped to defer or evade.

Whenever he came near the subject, he saw himself 35 years before, weeping into my mother's chenille robe, begging her to tell him that the rumors -- my father's flight, his irreversible departure -- were not true. He saw the hedges going untrimmed, the shingles on the house rotting and then falling off, the basement ruined by an incontinent dog, the illusion of family bliss irremediably shattered.

And in spite of all these ghosts, my brother had come to the same conclusion his father had: He could no longer live in the same house with his wife.

I wish I could say I was sanguine about this decision, or that I stood resolutely at my brother's side, supporting him in every barbed assault and eviscerating invective. The truth is, I was shamefully equivocal about the whole thing. To be a child of divorce is one burden. To watch another unfold is an acute form of torture, laced with poisonous memories. Misery to an adult is comprehensible, and even soluble. To a child, it is merely cruel and incomprehensible.

Nevertheless, my brother was resolute. As his sister, I am bound by blood to support him -- even if it meant distancing me from a sister-in-law I loved.

Divorce has become so common in American society that it is often viewed as just another pothole on the highway of contemporary life. So common are its features -- the single-parent household, the divorced-dad condos, the joint-custody juggling act -- that divorce has been declawed. The sidelong glances and collective shunning that my parents endured when they divorced in the early 1970s has been replaced by a collective shrug. Today, we have books about *The Starter Marriage*, as if the implosion of a first marriage is inevitable.

Statistics bear this out. Nearly 43 percent of marriages in the U.S. end in divorce, the federal government reports. The first years of a marriage are particularly vulnerable ones; one in three first marriages end within 10 years and one in five within 5 years. Today, a married couple with children is the exception rather than the norm.

There should be safety in numbers -- or at least some semblance of solace. Divorce shouldn't hurt my brother and sister-in-law as much as it does. But it is hurting them acutely and perhaps irremediably, largely because they are both children of divorce and intimately acquainted with its cruelty.

When my brother's chocolate brown eyes meet the wounded, familiar eyes of his 6-year-old son, the anguish is exquisitely familiar. It is, in fact, unbearable.

Unlike a marriage, divorce is excruciatingly lonely. Marriage, with its lavish drama and celebratory rituals, is lavish with witnesses and supporters. It's easy to forget that the reason we squeeze into uncomfortable, dazzling clothes and embrace a couple exchanging intimate assertions of fidelity, is to support and sustain their pledge.

So, when a couple unravels so fabulously, it is easy for family members like myself to feel a wee bit guilty.

It has not gone unnoticed by my family that my brother and sister-in-law have spent thousands of dollars on professional advice in an attempt to keep their marriage alive. I often wonder where the rest of us were during these pricey therapy sessions. Certainly, geography and employment have flung us into disparate quarters. But I remember my grandmother's quiet assertion that there was nothing that couldn't be solved with a cup of tea, a kitchen table and a little forbearance.

When my grandmother had inevitable travails with her volatile Irish husband, her sister Ruthie would come "up the house" for a cup of tea and sympathy. In the end, it was mended. It was not perfect, but it was endurable. Today, things seem less endurable, perhaps because the choices are too robust, or perhaps because children of fractious marriages will not tolerate such chronic irascibility in their own lives.

Oh, for a few Aunt Ruths, in their polyester pantsuits and sensible shoes. Heaven knows how many marriages they saved.

I, alas, saved none, in spite of my fervid entreaties. Now I am left to figure out how to sustain my beloved and bedraggled brother, my shattered and confused nephew and a sister-in-law I am supposed to excise from my life. It will be less of a struggle for me, than for him, to be sure. But a divorce's effect on a family is not limited to the couple whose marriage imploded. It sends shock waves throughout a fragile web, ripples that are deep and tenacious, and whose end is unknown.

In A World Of "Truthiness,"
A Bad Memory Is An Asset

I was going to write a memoir but I lost my memory. I used to think this was my downfall. Now I see it's an asset.

I figure with all these Baby Boomers skidding into senility, people won't be so picky about pesky little details like truth.

All that really counts when you're writing a memoir is that you have a bad life. Not just a crummy life, in which your mother constantly tells you you're fat and you failed driver's ed. But a real, bad, down-and-dirty life in which you match the sociopathic profile of Stalin but register somewhere between Little Dorrit and Heidi on the empathy scale.

The problem with James Frey is that his life wasn't bad enough.

Which is why he made it worse.

James Frey is the guy who wrote the memoir *A Million Little Pieces*, which recounts his scabrous tumble into drugs, alcohol and depravity. He was a drug-dealer, an addict, a drunk and a bum. Wanted in three states and covered, as he writes in the juicy opening paragraph, with "a colorful mixture of spit, snot, urine, vomit and blood," he is part Hunter S. Thompson and part Kurt Cobain, mad, bad and dangerous to know.

And all of that -- the drugs, the alcohol, the felony and even the bad writing -- we were willing to forgive, but for one thing. He was also a liar. And that's where we draw the line.

"It doesn't matter to me if it was all lies or not," wrote one reader on an addiction recovery Web site. "I read it (sic) I loved it (sic) It meant something to me. Would he read it if it was boring? NO. Would you read if it (sic) he talked about the boring days where he just sat around and smoked cigarettes. NO."

No, of course we wouldn't read it if he were just one dull, washed up pincushion. If he were just one, mutton-headed wretch like the rest of us, plodding around in the allergy relief aisle at Wal-Mart, picking his nose in traffic and staring off into oblivion at Blockbuster, who would care? Nobody will read a book about that. You got to sex it up with a little suicide and sex abuse, belt a cop or two, throw up on a VIP.

Did I mention it helps if your mother was a prostitute? Not mandatory, but it helps.

Remember the good old days when people used to write autobiographies and skip over the juicy parts? Churchill's memoirs are a nice bedtime read if you want to bone up on World War II, but they shed no light on his depression, obesity and penchant for (paging Dr. Freud) cigars.

And when Elizabeth Taylor finally found time to tell all, did she spill the beans on her seven husbands? No.

Instead we got *My Love Affair with Jewelry,* which, while more illuminating than *Nibbles and Me,* her teenage paean to her pet chipmunk, is all the light Liz has shed on her dramatic love life. Even a professional bad boy like Marlon Brando didn't disgorge the meaty decadence of his own notorious private life in *Songs My Mother Taught Me.* And W. Somerset Maugham? *Queer Eye* anyone?

In the good old days, people lied about their virtues instead of their vices. They went to Harvard. They pitched for the Yankees. They saved cats from burning buildings. They invented the Internet.

Today, the only way Bill Clinton could get re-elected is if he inhaled, snorted, shot up and freebased all while cruisin' cowboys on Brokeback Mountain.

Now you're only as good as your last indictment.

If Harriet Miers had been the abandoned lesbian love child of two Goths who died of hepatitis, nobody would have mewled about her modest intellect and predilection to over-accessorize. Supreme Court Justice would have been nothing. She would have made Oprah's Book Club.

Because making Oprah's Book Club a Who's Who of victimization is dependent on your having the most abject, bleak, incriminating, wrenching story ever told.

Even if it is a fake.

The Silent (Not) Majority

I am sitting on my suitcase at Boston's South Station and it is loud. I mean, really loud.

It is the Wednesday before Christmas, just after 5 p.m. The place is teeming with commuters galloping to train tracks, stuffing their faces with cranberry muffins and downing piping hot coffee grabbed from the Starbucks across the way.

Just outside, a brass quintet is playing gorgeous Baroque music to the apparent enjoyment of no one in particular. And a lone postal agent has set up shop in the middle of the station, grabbing late packages from panting consumers eager to make the Christmas deadline. A guy behind the clerk is hawking Johnny Damon pictures for half-price. Damon has just been shorn, shaved and traded to the Yankees, which is filling this arena, anyway, with a familiar bitterness. "So much for loyalty," a guy quips, striding angrily by.

But Johnny Damon is not my concern. Getting home is, but it is coupled with an effort to maintain my slowly deteriorating composure.

Travel in America is always fraught with frenzy, of course. But I'm beginning to believe that engaging in any sort of public assembly, from the DMV to the shopping mall, is worse than drudgery. It has become a farrago of disappointment and indignation, an exercise in misanthropy. Nothing confirms one's right to hate one's fellow man quite like an immersion in a crowded public space.

"Listen to me, listen to me!" a woman is shouting into her cell phone. The woman is short and bovine, with low-heeled galoshes and a practical if lumpish winter hat. She is pacing in circles like a tigress and her indignation is mounting with every step. "He said he didn't want to be interrupted," she growls, "but this time, this time, when it's me, you see, when it's me, this time, I'm supposed to interrupt him!"

The woman is bellowing and her consonants are thwacking against each other like bowling pins. She is spitting, literally, into the air and the more she shouts, the more guttural and demonic her tirade becomes.

Why don't cell phones ever go dead when you want them to?

Cell phones, whose popularity rests on their convenience, have introduced us to two new kinds of incivility. The first, of course, is the blatant discourtesy of loudmouth users who assault anyone in their perimeter with the inanity of their blather. The second is the equally unsettling revelation that people speak to one another with discourtesy, disrespect and a dismissiveness that makes you wonder if the only reason people talk to one another is to stave off boredom.

Now I have two words I want to say to this woman: "Shut Up." But I do not say them. I do not say this because I am a civil person. I do not say this because I'm determined to rise above my atavistic urge to impale her with my cuticle stick.

I do not say this because I do not want to become like her.

And there it is, isn't it? The reason that the civil don't revolt against the insolent is that they are girded by a sense of integrity that tells them such rudeness is beneath them. Then, of course, there's the possibility that they might be killed. This woman, for instance, looks like she purees colleagues for lunch.

Increasingly, public spaces have become a showcase for bad behavior. The concept of shame has gone the way of the 8-track, replaced by the far-more inspiring notion of self-righteousness. Faced with such a cacophony of rudeness, a growing silent majority is beginning to opt out of the public sphere altogether.

This year, consumer spending on-line increased between 25 and 30 percent. Part of that is the increasing comfort level with the Internet, but part of that has to be people like me who cannot abide jostling with other pajama-wearing, foul-mouthed patrons.

Attendance at movies has decreased more than 7 percent in the United States, the third year in a row Hollywood has suffered declining numbers at the box office. That could be because Hollywood is delivering a lousy product, but rentals of DVDs are up 14 percent. People want to see movies, they just don't want to spend $10 to be drop-kicked into some stranger's den.

Meanwhile, Nielsen Media Research reported that the average U.S. home watched more TV during the 2004-05 season than in any other season since they began monitoring TV viewing in the 1950s. The average adult watched 8 hours, 11 minutes of TV daily. TV might be lousy, but at least you don't have to leave home to watch it. Indeed, one of the most popular Web sites going is NetFlix, which allows consumers to order DVDs without having to bother with the rabble at the local video store.

Technology is allowing us to bypass human interaction altogether. I used to think that was bad for society. Now I see it as a refuge for the silent majority like me, whose evil stares are as futile and unsatisfying as a slap across the face with a glove.

What's Up Doc? The Raunch Factor
In Children's Films

When my son turned 2, a generous relative gave him a copy of the movie, "Shrek."

"It's hysterical," said the chirpy relative. "You'll love it, too."

Well, I did. Sort of.

"Shrek," like its cousins "Dr. Doolittle," "Finding Nemo," and "Monsters, Inc." are marketed to kids, with the gentle suggestion that adults will enjoy them, too. And you will enjoy them, particularly if you loved "Blazing Saddles," "Porkys" and "Animal House."

Don't get me wrong. "Shrek" is a funny movie with a redemptive message about the power of love. But in its unapologetic vulgarity, it is emblematic of the crassness and incivility of children's movies that has gone virtually unnoticed by the country's self-appointed finger-waggers. While the religious right is busy fulminating about which Teletubby is the gay, and assailing PBS for including gay parents on one of its most popular children's programs, the real threat to children's sensibilities goes unchecked.

Earlier this year, Warner Brothers introduced a meaner, leaner Bugs Bunny, a raging rodent whose beloved buck teeth now look like two glinting bayonets. The retooling of the wry sophisticate into a rampaging warrior is part of an updated Looney Toons series called "Loonatics," set in the year 2772. Those affably daffy vaudevillians have gone the way of Lassie. No kid worth his weight in Game Boys is going to buy a Shakespeare-quoting bunny rabbit. That is, like, so yesterday.

"Sexual content seems to be of more concern than gratuitous violence," Marsha Williams, a vice president for research at Nickelodeon told *The New York Times*. But while parents debate which is worse, violence or sex a more subtle, but arguably more pervasive, threat stalks the nation's youth. It's incivility.

Listen, for a moment, to the way characters talk to one another in top-grossing "family" films like "Shrek" and "Dr. Doolittle."

"Two words," the ogre Shrek says to his companion, the Donkey, "Shut. Up."

Two words that you would likely not want your child to use, and two words that have become all too commonplace in movies from "Toy Story," to "Shrek." It is not merely those two words, but a whole manner of speaking to one another that is less articulate, less civil and generally more coarse than the days of "Sleeping Beauty" or "Bambi."

"Excuse me," says Shrek, to a put-upon Princess Fiona, "I have to save my ass."

Funny. Funny to an adult who understands the double-entendre. But does a 5-year-old understand that? Should they? Ever since Bart Simpson made it OK and even hip to say "This sucks," absolutely everything sucks, from chicken nuggets to "Chicken Run." Mean people suck, says a popular bumper sticker. School sucks, says a popular Web site that sells term papers to desperate students.

Just as advertisements directed at children bank on a more adversarial relationship between parents and children, so, too, children's films today celebrate a sharp-edged antagonism between characters. Sarcasm is the *lingua franca* of children's movies today, sullying the dialog and sending the not-too-subtle message that he who comes up with the most smart-ass remark wins the day.

And then there are the, ahem, poop jokes.

Scatological humor has become the mainstay of most children's movies, meaning that a parent is likely to endure more jokes about flatulence, to say nothing of flatulence itself, at home than any frazzled working mother has any right to endure.

"Man, you gotta warn somebody before you just crack one off like that," the Donkey says to Shrek, as he follows the ogre up a mountain. "My mouth was open and everything."

All right. It's funny. But what message does it send to children about humor? As Mark Schone lamented last year in *The Boston Globe*, "Now you can't watch a kids' flick without stepping in poop. Potty humor has become *de rigueur* for movies aimed at children."

Schone cites movies like "Dr. Doolittle," in which Eddie Murphy's character wrinkles his nose as he treats a rat for a gas attack. In the new "101 Dalmatians," a puppy named Whizzer pees on a picture of Cruella De Ville.

All of this leads to a crasser, less civil environment in which what we say to one another is judged not by its courtesy but by its derisiveness. How we speak to one another is the foundation on which we build social behavior. When it is spoiled by nasty slurs and sharp-edged digs at people supposed to be our friends we have no one to blame but ourselves when our children haul off and crack us.

Trapped In His Body,
Longing To Play It Again

Bob Veillette doodled.

In the endless news meetings that held us captive at the Waterbury, Conn., newspaper at which we worked, he scribbled geometric honeycombs on plain white paper, the effect something of a hybrid of M.C. Escher and Sol LeWitt. I used to wonder where his mind went in those abstracted sketches he made. Perhaps to the Shakespeare stanzas he had memorized, or the construction of jazz harmonies he conceived on piano.

The question has become more poignant now; nearly a year and a half after Bob was felled by a massive stroke, which left him fully aware, but mute and paralyzed, imprisoned in his own skin. The stroke hit his brain stem, a kind of neural funnel that pours the brain's impulses into the spinal cord. Disabled, it leaves the mind blisteringly aware and the body utterly lifeless; hence, its name, "locked-in-syndrome."

Bob's Poe-like condition is the same that afflicted Jean-Dominique Bauby, the French editor of *Elle*, whose book, *The Diving Bell and the Butterfly*, has now been made into a film by Julian Schnabel. Bob, too, was an editor, at the *Republican-American*, the paper with which he grew up and spent nearly 30 years. Bauby's book was "dictated," by blinking his left eye, a system in which I have become painfully proficient. Bob's former speech, an animated ramble that he peppered with Shakespearean quotes like "a good deed in a naughty world" and "with malice toward none," has been reduced to a series of eye movements. His visitor recites a series of letters "E, T, A, O, I," used most frequently in the English language. When the visitor arrives at a letter Bob desires, he raises his cerulean blue eyes.

It is a laborious process, and I have learned to curb my temptation to guess. ("Revolt? Is the word revolt, Bob?") Often, as I jot a long-arrived-at letter onto a yellow legal pad, I remember the lightening liquidity of Bob's fingers on the computer keyboard, a movement hauntingly reminiscent of his fingers on his piano keyboard, the place where he felt most at home and most alive.

Bill Evans, Dave McKenna, Art Tatum. These were lions to Bob, jazz geniuses along the lines of Chopin, whom he could not listen to without feeling his own inadequacy. I cannot play a lick of piano, but I was an attentive and appreciative audience member and Bob accepted with delectation the recordings I copied for him, explaining the delicate points of jazz with an animation and precision that enlightened and engaged me. I had not understood what the "stride piano" of Marian MacPartland was before. But I now visualize Bob's simulation of it whenever I hear her play.

Bob and I are both Catholics, and have a catechist's predilection for memorization. But I was no match for Bob's fluency with Shakespeare, whole passages of which he would recite as nimbly as if it were the Nicene Creed. There were deeper divisions in our approach to our faith. I am an avid, though clumsy reader of theology, a discipline Bob adamantly dismissed. "I question everything else in my life," he told me. "My faith," and here he slapped his heart. "My faith is something I never question." I was irritated at his dismissal, and then envious. I longed for Bob's ability to make the thorny more basic.

O, that this too, too solid flesh would melt/thaw and resolve itself into the dew/or that the everlasting had not set his hand against self-slaughter.

On the day that I learned of Bob's stroke, a colleague, dissolving in tears, blurted, "I'd rather he was hit by a truck."

I believe my colleague was thinking of Bob's restless energy, of his strapping physicality, of his long runs and hypnotizing hours at the piano. But after a year and a half of Bob's physical imprisonment, I have learned that the soul is a plucky, persistent beast. When the Terry Schiavo case was being debated, I remember Bob making an unplugging motion with his arms. "If it were me, zip," he said.

And then suddenly it was him. And, defiantly, he wanted to live.

When your brain stem has been wounded, surprisingly, there are two things you can still do. You can cry. And you can laugh. In the early days of his illness, when he realized the paralysis was irreversible, Bob cried a lot -- long, wounded howls of anguish that would dissolve a stoic. Today, I tell him stories about the newsroom, and he laughs. Oh, his laughs are messy and contorted, but they are gorgeous.

"I bear my cross ruefully, and with grace," he told me. The mind flies to all manner of imaginary heavens, I have learned. Bob's flies often back to the piano, where he dreams he is playing again, a favorite song we both can recite by heart:

Funny, I should have saved those left-over tears
Funny, but here's that rainy day
Here's that rainy day
I told you about
And I laughed at the thought
that it might turn out that way.

St Paul, The Messenger, Misunderstood

When I told a friend that I had named my son after St. Paul, she had an arch reaction.

"Why would you name your son after that misogynist?" she said.

I was prepared for that. Whether invoking Paul's imprecation that "wives must be submissive to their husbands," (Ephesians 5: 22-23) or that Jews "killed both the Lord Jesus and the prophets," (Thessalonians 2:15), Paul of Tarsus has been the fall guy for every iniquity from misogyny to anti-Semitism.

And yet this year, the 2,000th anniversary of his birth, the Vatican is celebrating "the year of St. Paul," by encouraging Catholics to re-examine Paul, the most influential shaper of Christianity outside of Jesus. How far this will go in reshaping the conventional wisdom about Paul will depend on how far the church is willing to go to bring new, more nuanced scholarship about this exhilarating -- and exasperating -- man into the pews.

From Andre Gide, to Thomas Jefferson, to George Bernard Shaw, the devout and the doubtful have taken aim at Paul, dismissing him as the wet blanket of the New Testament, a rigid, chauvinistic scold who took all the Good out of the Good News and replaced in with a dour, censorious bleakness. Jefferson called Paul the "first corrupter of the doctrines of Jesus." Nietzsche said that the evangelist had "a genius for hatred."

Paul, the first and most vigorous of theologians, has been the most maligned, misunderstood and misrepresented saint in Christian history. And yet I chose to name my son after him because I believe Paul best articulates the electrifying possibilities of humankind and the ecstatic contradictions that make it so difficult to achieve them. I love the very qualities that have vexed so many: Paul's volatility, his gusto, his self-lacerating disappointment in himself and his fiery invectives against those who he believes diminish Jesus' message. If Paul is vicious in his condemnation of the wicked, he can at least be credited for lumping himself in that group.

As historian Henry Bamford Parkes wrote, "Emotional and excitable, alternating between states of ecstasy and depression, utterly convinced of his guidance by the Spirit and given to boasting of his own achievements, utterly convinced of his guidance by the Spirit..Paul revealed his whole personality with an astonishing candor and sincerity. His letters were the earliest example of that full acceptance of naked humanity not as it ought to be, but as it was..."

Part of the problem for Paul is that his letters are a response to first-century crisis about which we know next to nothing. As Garry Wills writes in *What Paul Meant*, "We hear his raised voice without knowing what the other side was shouting." The second problem, as Georgetown University Professor Anthony Tambasco told me, is that "some of the text that Paul gets blamed for, he probably didn't write."

Of the 13 letters attributed by Paul, only seven are now accepted as certainly his. Letters like those to Timothy and Titus, for instance, were clearly not written by Paul. They were written at a time when the church had become more systematized -- and patriarchal. Hence: "Let a woman learn in silence with full submission. I permit no woman to teach or have authority over a man, she is to keep silent" (Timothy 2:11-13) was almost certainly not written by Paul.

"Paul had people who he called fellow apostles and they were women," said Tambasco, author of *In The Days of Paul*.

The problem is while Paul writes memorably that "in Christ there is neither male nor female" (Galatians 3:28), he nevertheless believes, as Harold W. Attridge, Dean of Yale Divinity School, told me, "There's also the natural order of things that needs to be respected." And that was a first-century social order.

"There were some people in Paul's school and tradition who took that impulse in Paul rather strictly," Attridge said. "So the passage that talks about women not to take leadership roles or to teach in the church are probably not by Paul."

Paul's alleged anti-Semitism is a bit more subtle. As a bridge between Judaism and Christianity, Paul wrestles deeply with the necessity to keep all of Jewish ritual, including circumcision, or whether the risen Jesus is "the saving reality" and that the law, as Tambasco says "is God's second best gift." It's fine to keep it, Paul says, but don't impose it on non-Jews. Later Christians, of course, used this and other scriptural readings to bolster a raging anti-Semitism, the vestiges of which are tenacious.

But the Paul I love best is the Paul who wrestles with his own failings and finds healing in God's grace. "I do not understand my own actions," he laments in Romans. For I do not do what I want, but I do the very thing I hate...For I do not the good I want, but the evil I do not want is what I do. (Romans: 7-15-16; 18-20). This is a man who admits he is clumsy at devotion "we do not know how to pray as we ought, but that very Spirit intercedes for us with sighs too deep for words."

Is Paul harsh? Sure he is. But he is also gloriously poetic, recognizing that despite humanity's failings, it is trussed irrevocably to God.

"For I am convinced," he writes in Romans, "that neither death, nor life, nor angels, nor rulers, nor things present, nor things to come, nor powers, nor height, nor depth, nor anything else in all creation, will be able to separate us from the love of God in Christ Jesus our Lord."

Computer's Memory Is The First To Go

I ordered more memory the other day. But the postman forgot to bring it. Or maybe the supplier forgot to send it.

I don't remember.

The memory I bought was for my computer, a now-archaic little laptop that I purchased in 2001. Or maybe it was 2000.

Anyway, I bought the memory because I want the computer to work faster, which, of course, is the whole point of having a computer. Otherwise, I could use my reliable Royal typewriter, if I could remember where I put it.

Why memory relates to speed and not to space is not something I completely understand. But what I have learned in my futile attempt to join the 21st century is that the lexicon of computers is laden with incongruities, memory being the least of them. For instance, there are hard drives and soft ware and chips, which come in bytes, or maybe bites, or maybe just morsels. There are RAMs, which shouldn't be confused with ROMs, and MP3s, which shouldn't be confused with the British Secret Service, MI5. Or was that the name of their Mars probe? I can't remember.

Then there's this whole cosmology of very large numbers with comic-book-like names like mega, giga and kilo, who together form the Justice League of Acronyms. Hertz, of course, refers to speed, which makes sense to anyone who remembers O.J. before he hooked up with Nicole.

Keeping track of all these logarithms requires a lot of memory. Or maybe that's disc space. It's hard to keep track.

If you really need to understand this, you have to ask a teenage boy. It is always good to come armed with "Return of the King" tickets and say you believe J.R.R. Tolkien should have received the Nobel Prize for literature.

The teenage boy will say something to you like, "You only have 64 RAMs?"

At which point, you say, "Is that bad?"

To which he will likely say, "Whatever."

I've been thinking a lot about this memory predicament because of some recent breakthroughs in the field of neuroscience, which were really fascinating. If, of course, I could remember them.

The research has to do with how we store -- or in the medical lexicon "reconsolidate" -- memory. It appears that memory is only as good as your last bout of nostalgia. Memory is particularly vulnerable when a person recalls it and then stores it away for future use.

This partially explains what my husband refers to as "Irish garnish," in which stories retold are never retold the same way. Every time the story is told, a little ornament is added, a trifling detail (like the truth) eliminated and the story made more dramatic and captivating than it was on first telling.

It turns out that this process is not unique to the Irish but that it has to do with neurobiology. Permanent memory, as Carey Goldberg wrote recently in *The Boston Globe*, "is not only vulnerable to change, but becomes vulnerable every time it is called to mind."

It appears that certain proteins are needed to place memories back into storage after they are called up.

In computer terms, something happens when the brain hits the "save" function of its circuitry that puts that memory at risk.

Sometimes, that's a positive development. Not all memories are pleasant.

And, as Dr. Richard A. Friedman wrote in *The New York Times*, traumatic events are stored in the amygdala, an older part of the brain that matures faster than the newer (in evolutionary terms) part of the brain, the hippocampus.

That's why we tend to remember the frightening and menacing parts of even our early life, while all those wonderfully benign, cooing moments of baby-hood get flushed down the neurobiological sewer.

Or, in computer terms, deleted.

It's not clear to me whether my laptop memory will be any better than my biological one.

All I know is that it will be a lot faster, which seems somehow beside the point.

My new memory has yet to be delivered, a month after I ordered it. At wits end, I called Gateway, my computer company, to complain.

"Hey," I said, "What the Dell?"

The Gateway operator said she needed my order number to respond.

Naturally, I forgot it.

Why Mom Wants To Dry Your Hair

My mother wants to blow dry my hair.

"I'm perfectly capable of blow-drying my own hair, Mom."

My mother and I are standing in one of those hotel bathrooms with the too-strong fluorescent lights and the bite-size toiletries. We're attending a family function in a far-away city, and family members have been braiding their way through the connecting rooms on a floor we have appropriated, borrowing cosmetics, socks and hair dryers.

"I know," my mother says, pouting into the mirror. "I just want to do it."

I look down at my mother, who stands just under my shoulder blades. She's mesmerized by the reflection of the two of us in the mirror. I can see her mentally appraising our features and counting up the ones that belong to her: Same mouth, same hair, father's eyes, grandfather's nose.

"Think people would know we're related?" she asks.

I look at her short, squat frame, the dark skin, the caramel eyes, the wide mouth and perfect teeth. "Not a chance," I say, dipping into the hair gel. She smirks.

"I love watching people dry their hair," says my mother. "It's like watching a fire. You know, you just get kind of hypnotized."

I shake my head. Despite a lifetime of experience with my mother's impulsive declarations and wobbly theories, she can still throw me off guard. A few weeks ago, I walked into her house and she was curled up on the sofa with a Tupperware bowl full of popcorn on her stomach and two perching cats on each thigh, half-watching one of those treacly made-for-TV movies. "What's this?" I said, pointing to the television.

"I have no idea," she said, popping kernels into her mouth. "I just love movies. I sit. I watch. I have no idea what they're about."

It is moments like that that make me question my DNA composition. How can you watch a movie and not know what it is about? Isn't that cognitively impossible? I run the hotel hair dryer over my damp hair as my mother stares narcotically into the mirror. I wonder: If the two of us were thrown into the gaggle of panty-hosed, cosmetically entombed, atomized women chicken-dancing in the banquet hall downstairs, would anybody imagine we grew up eating off the same Corelle?

"Let me try," my mother pleads.

"You'll make me all poofy," I say.

I should know; there have been precedents.

On the Friday nights of my girlhood, my mother washed my hair in a deep, porcelain tub of a kitchen sink. I remember staring into the stainless-steel water stopper that was salted with scraps of food and tiny Brillo pad hairs. My hair was long then and washing it was an ordeal, but one my mother relished. "You could be a Playboy bunny with hair like that," my mother used to say. Good grief: Every mother's dream.

On those very Catholic Friday nights, my mother brought red-and-white paper cartons from the fish market at the top of the street. Breaded fish for my brothers; crinkled French fries and chicken noodle soup for me. The scent of the fish and the grease of the fries mingled into a tawny-colored, briny perfume that wafted over the four of us as we sat at the table, me with my hair under a turban-tied towel. From underneath the sink, my mother pulled a pink Sunbeam hair dryer, setting it by the napkin beside me. Dexterously, she pulled my hair under its billowy flowered net. It was thus that I ate my Friday french fries and chicken noodle soup, the whiny hum of the hair dryer pelting my reddening ears, the scent of fish and fries and soup mixing with the aluminum tang of the hair dryer, the muffled words of my brothers and mother folding symphonically into the night.

When dinner was over and my hair dried, my mother disengaged the hair dryer and brushed my hair 100 times with a black bristled brush. She collected it into a pony tail and swept it into a bouffant. She gathered it like a scarf around my neck; she dampened it again, coiled it in ringlets and ironed it dry, the heat steaming off the curls like hot pasta. "Can I just go to bed now," I whined. "No," she said. "I'm playing." And she would play like that until I nodded off to sleep: her living doll, her would-be Playboy bunny.

Not long ago, I went to see "The Winter Guest," a movie about a mother who tries vainly to comfort her independent-minded daughter, who is bereft over the death of her husband. In a fit of frustration over the cloying behavior of her mother, the daughter screams, "I don't need you." The mother is thunderstruck. "Don't ever say that. It was you who taught me to be needed."

I think about that as my mother watches in admiration and in need, perhaps recalling those same Friday nights, perhaps recalling others lost to my memory, when the communion we had was through a black bristled brush and pink Sunbeam hair dryer. I wonder what it is like to have a daughter whose looks you nourish, but, in the end, cannot control. When, I wonder, do you give up the brush? When do you stop telling her to get the hair out of her eyes? When do you stop making her into the doll you always wanted? And what does it feel like to give that up?

I click off the hair dryer and hand the brush to my mother. "All right," I say. "Give it your best shot."

The Hearth Is A Lonely Hunter

Once upon a time, I worked for a woman named Mrs. Miller, who was a slob. Her slovenliness was, in fact, the core of our relationship. Mrs. Miller paid me to clean her house, a task as hopeless as it was bleak. I had cleaned many houses in my teenage years, bicycling from house to house with a backpack soggy with Lysol and Scrubbing Bubbles. I usually left these assignments swelled with the virtuous blush of tidiness. Sinks gleamed; floors shined; faucets sparkled; I was a dazzling success at bringing order to a disordered world.

But Mrs. Miller eluded my meticulous labors. A chubby, arthritic, affable old lady who stacked magazines, boxes, wrapping paper and linens in a chaotic collage of clutter that made navigating through her house nearly impossible, Mrs. Miller resisted my industrious scouring with an ingenuous resolve. "No dear," she would say gently, when I suggested assembling brickyards worth of *Ladies Home Journals* in a Rubbermaid container. "I may need a recipe in there, and I like them where I can see them."

This wasn't easy to take.

There were some days when I had to squelch any urge to tell Mrs. Miller that what she needed was a front-end loader and a match.

Mrs. Miller seemed oblivious to my barely suppressed horror. She would thread her way through her drifts of debris, with an earnest, unflappable purpose, known to her alone. I was never alone in her house. She followed me like a dog.

Passing mothball-scented columns of quilts, shoe boxes stacked like enormous Legos and newspaper columns that drooped like cobwebs from the furniture, Mrs. Miller would lead me to one lonely, neglected corner, to which together we would bring order.

Why this corner, or why these fermenting jelly glasses, I never knew. But wandering through this filth was a nostalgic adventure for Mrs. Miller. And I was her personal Beatrice, lighting her way through an inferno of chaos.

It did not take long for me to discover that what Mrs. Miller really wanted was not to have her toilets glisten, nor her mantle swell with the lemony balm of Old English polish. It did not matter to Mrs. Miller that I discovered tiny brown pellets in her linen closet, obvious evidence of mice. Or that her collection of sand would impress few who managed to machete their way to her squalid living room. Mrs. Miller had hired me to clean her house, but in the six years I worked for her it never was. What Mrs. Miller needed was not my dust cloth, but me.

I thought of Mrs. Miller recently when I heard that the Chore Service had escaped an early death. The Chore Service, which began in 1992, provides services for the elderly in nine Litchfield County towns. That includes tasks like grocery shopping, vacuuming and yard work. In substance, if not in spirit, it provides very much the same type of assistance I provided Mrs. Miller 25 years ago. Granted, wielding a weed-whacker is a long way from brandishing a toilet brush and Soft Scrub, but in human terms, it is very much the same.

For many senior citizens relying on Chore Service, the peal of a doorbell that announces assistance offers more than visible benefits. It can be their only contact with the outside world.

When I worked for Mrs. Miller, she didn't technically live alone. She lived with her husband and son, two shadowy presences whom I knew only through her vivid and chagrined description of them. Her husband, whom she met on a rail excursion, seemed a methodical, distant, censorious man who did not share his wife's affection for literature and antiques. Her son, Timmy, appeared to be an overfed, overindulged failure. His continued presence in her house was a clear disappointment to Mrs. Miller, who lamented his lack of luck in romance.

Much of Mrs. Miller's life was a lament, an elegy to missed opportunities and unmet expectations. She had wanted to be a writer and infrequently penned an antique column for the local newspaper. She typed it out on the gun-metal Olivetti typewriter that sat on the buffet, next to her toaster oven. Streams of these observations curled out of the sewing basket she stuffed between her recliner and ottoman. She was keen on sharing them with me.

In spite of her clear incapacity for cleanliness, I grew enamored of and even sympathetic to Mrs. Miller's plight. The flotsam that filled her cramped rooms clearly filled an emotional void. Often, while I ironed hopelessly outdated curtains and white crumpled sheets dappled with rust, she would pull up her nut-brown hassock and sit beside me, rhapsodizing about the wedding gifts she had received 45 years before, the avocado curtains she peered out of awaiting her son's return from school, the apron she tied around her then-tiny waist as she prepared her young family's meals.

That she still had these things had, at first, filled me with consternation. I steeled myself for the day I would insist that she discard them. But I grew to see that they were tangible shards of a soul. And I saw that her conversations with me, despite their pretense of purpose, availed her of a communion that had been denied her. Loneliness is a silent scourge. It is a dreary business, and bleaker still when it festers in families.

For six years, I left Mrs. Miller's cluttered home feeling I had failed her. Now that she is gone, long dead, the memories of her desperate prattle still so vivid, I see that she got what she paid for.

The Birds Lend Grace
To A French Nightmare

ANGERS, FRANCE

Monsieur takes care of the birds. In the morning, just after dawn, he moistens the spoils of last night's bread in his fist. He pads out into the garden in his bright blue overalls and sets the cottony bread in a sardine tin. The sardine tin is his own invention. He nailed it, like a porch, to the outside of the lacquered wood house he built for the birds. Next to it, a plastic silo gobbles the spoonfuls of seed Monsieur feeds it. By the time noon spreads over the pebbled garden, the pillow of bread will be shredded and sunflower seeds will dot Monsieur's delphinium bed.

From the terrace, I watch the birds flock around my French "father" like a shadow. I have returned to this town, where I was lodged by Monsieur and his wife in 1983, to see this again. Watching Monsieur, a tiny man with a toothless smile and a leathery face, is like watching waves lap up against the shore for me. It is that predictable, that refreshing. "Ah, Tracey," he says. "You see how demanding these birds are! They're never satisfied. Worse than a wife!" Monsieur laughs phlegmatically and pats me hard on the back. He is the size of an elf but as strong as a bull, his chest expansive and taut, his waist narrow, his sinewy legs bowed and bruised. He is a small man, with a small house and a small garden, on whose roost small birds come to rest. Including, as often as possible, me.

More than 50 years ago, Monsieur went to make his name in Paris. He was a butcher's son, trained to slaughter. He squeezed the life out of chickens and slit the throats of cows. In 1941, the year he left, Paris was suffering a different death. Nazis had spread through the boulevards like a cancer. Occupied Paris inhaled fear and exhaled apprehension, but it kept breathing.

It might have kept on this way, but the Nazis grew increasingly desperate. By 1943 Germany was losing men by the tankful. The Nazis needed laborers to run their war machine. They took Monsieur.

In February of 1943, Monsieur was arrested and deported to Berlin. For 24 months, he nourished the Nazi war machine with his sweat. In the morning, the S.S. marched him four kilometers to a factory where, for 12 hours, he fed bucket after bucket of coal into the hot, thirsty throat of a furnace. When he describes this, he does not do it in words. He stands up. He marches. He lifts an invisible bucket. He throws it into an invisible furnace. He accents his pantomime with disgust. He has lost one vocal cord to cancer, but with the other he forces language through his windpipe. And he says it over and over again. "Twenty-four months. Twenty-four months."

At the end of the day, he was given a bowl of soup.

When he talks about the soup, he might as well be talking about vomit. It would be generous to call it soup. It was garbage floating in hot water.

When finally the Allies stormed Berlin, he counted 380 shellings in one day. At gunpoint, he was forced to continue working. Fellow workers fell beside him. Roofs caved in. Buildings were leveled.

After Germany surrendered, Monsieur walked along the one train line leading back to France until he nearly withered. Within three years, doctors would remove three-quarters of his stomach, ulcerated due to malnutrition. Today, he eats slowly, slicing Camembert on the tarnished blade of his slim jackknife and spreading it across his bread.

"Tracey," he says to me, pointing his jackknife. "This is what hate will do. This is what war will bring."

Monsieur tells us his story as dusk cloaks the garden. Outside, the swallows have stopped their crepuscular stroll, and I suffocate in the silence of regret. I do not know what to say to Monsieur. Every word seems sterile and inept. I tell him the truth: that I had no idea so many French were deported -- 600,000 total -- to work in Nazi factories. He receives no recompense for such suffering, and no military pension, since he was a prisoner, not a military man.

On the train leaving Angers, his blue eyes turn pink with tears as he embraces me. He will be 80 this September and I do not know when I will see him again.

Under the sterile blue light of my computer screen at home, I search the Internet for information about men like Monsieur. The Internet seems parched of such information, and I am incredulous that these stories are so seldom heard. But then I see the news that a Belgian woman, deported to work for the Nazis, has successfully sued the German government for wages earned. I see a figure, $7,789. I print the document. I will send this to Monsieur, I think. It may give him hope.

But the evening after I posted the document, regret swallows me. I have given an American Band-Aid to a French nightmare. The money is insignificant, and my suggestion insulting. I sit on my deck and soak in self-recrimination.

In the pine tree, a sparrow family perches on our store-bought birdhouse. It peeps and flutters and I remember Monsieur swallowed by hungry birds, bathing their font in moist bread.

I know neither the path to forgiveness nor the trail to forgetting. I only know that to be bewitched by serenity after horror takes a courage foreign to my American mind. I can only listen to the symphony of the birds, imagining Monsieur in a halo of sparrows, teaching me that life, like bird feeding, can be canopied, in the most ordinary moments, by unaccountable grace.

Can't Help Singing Dat Song Of Hers

My mother will be singing on Mother's Day. As she has sung on a thousand other Mother's Days. As she will probably do as long as there are Mother's Days, or mothers, or songs. For my mother has always been a singer and so I have grown up around songs.

In my youth, I took this profession for granted. Some girls' mothers worked in bakeries and dressed in white aprons and brought them home brownies. Some girls' mothers worked in hospitals and dressed in white nylons and were useful when you fell out of trees. But my mother worked in nightclubs and dressed in black gowns with shiny rhinestones and brought back Dinah Shore and Sophie Tucker. It was not practical, but it was lyrical.

And my mother has made no bones about which she considers preeminent. "You have to follow your heart, pumpkin," she used to tell me, slapping on makeup as I set mesmerized on the edge of the tub. "You can't ignore a talent; that'd be like spitting in God's face."

My mother had her own theology, cobbled from the Catholicism of her youth to the lyrics of Johnny Mercer to the pages of *Jonathan Livingstone Seagull*. It was not the Nicene Creed, to be sure, but it was always engaging, if infrequently consistent. My mother is a sandwich of Auntie Mame, Bette Midler and Liza Minnelli, with a dash of Donna Reed. If one opened the closet of my mother's bedroom, one risked being beaned by a tambourine, a set of maracas and a feather boa. Well, my mother liked props.

"Rhinestones and black, sweetie; they're a performer's bread and butter," she said. Together, we roamed the consignment shops of greater Boston, ransacking racks of clothes that smelled of moth balls and cigarettes, and, to me, looked like some one's old drapes.

"But this would look faah-bulous on stage," my mother would say, a tad too loudly, attracting the attention of the rest of the patrons.

Few people knew an actual cabaret singer and my mother was glad to be their first. That opportunity was not always greeted enthusiastically, "So," said a friend's father, after pronouncing a blessing on his meatloaf and folding his hands piously, "is your mother still singing in bars?" I could only look quizzically in his direction and imagine what kind of lurid images he must have had of my mother, swilling whiskey in the saloons of Boston in some shimmering negligee like Marlene Dietrich. I could no more tell him that it was not quite like that as picture him singing "Fever" at his Monday prayer meeting.

My neighbor's sneering only provided additional comic material for my mother, who spared no mercy in her good-natured indictment of suburban hypocrisy. My neighbors told their children not to care what other people thought about them. But together, they dressed in the same clothes, bought the same Impalas, ate the same crullers and not-so-furtively whispered about the goings-on of the *louche* family down the street.

My mother dressed in a black sweat suit with fat white stars outlined in pink beads. "I got a lot of nerve going out like this," she said, gunning the Pinto meatily down the street. My mother combined maternity and entertainment in an alchemy of affection that embraced as it puzzled. When I was a girl, her voice would rise from the basement, where she vocalized while folding laundry, up through the heating vents into the oxygen of my girlhood, like heat, like air, like motherhood itself. In this ersatz intercom system, I would hear her ballads, the sound following me throughout the house like a shadow. "Fish gotta swim; birds gotta fly/ I gotta love one man 'til I die/can't help lovin' dat man of mine," she would sing, as she folded underwear and matched socks and set the Maytag on spin.

From this I learned that song could be everywhere, that a lullaby could be soft or gentle or breezy or bombastic. And every day, each moment, had its own lyric, its own heat.

Of course, my mother short-changed us on certain things. I cannot cook, nor take up a hem, nor get that sharp crease in the arm of a shirt. I have no idea how long asparagus keeps or when the chicken is fully baked. But I have Gershwin and Mercer and Berlin, and though I have been to operas, and concerts and symphonies and ballets, nothing to me is as mesmerizing as one singer and one piano. And if that singer is my mother, and the voice on the gust of air her own, then I am in love, with life, with music and with the voice that gave my life its lyric.

Friends, Rivals And Heartbreak

My son has a rival. Another boy, a clever little tot of 6, has stolen the claims to the heart of PJ's best friend, Michael. "He's the complete opposite of me," sighed PJ. "He likes baseball; I like soccer. He likes sauce on his pasta. I don't like sauce on my pasta."

Such dissonance cannot be bridged, clearly, and so PJ has found himself in the discomfiting position of vying for the attention of a boy he has known since the cradle. Alas, he has no fight in him.

Holding my hand in the moonlight, as we walk the dog, PJ confides that Michael spent all of their play date preoccupied with this interloper, while PJ was left to scour Michael's toy chest unimpeded.

"Did you ask Michael to include you in their games?" I ask.

PJ's eyes begin to leak. "I was too sad," he says.

"PJ, I'm sure if you talk to Michael and explain how it hurts you to be excluded, he'll include you," I say. "He's your best friend. He doesn't want to hurt you."

"But I heard them talking," mewls PJ. "They said they were very, very best friends."

And then it happens. The flood of tears that I am helpless to stop, precipitated by an emotion that is so old and so exquisitely painful that I am left merely mute, rubbing my son's hand in recognition.

Everyone has a best friend, I suppose, and I have had many, and that does seem rather shameful. After all, a best friend implies some sort of indissoluble contract, something like the oath Jeanie Collins and I made on the railroad tracks

38 years ago, which we sealed with a mixing of our blood, oozing copiously out of our thumbs. We had pricked them with a baby blue safety pin from her brother's diaper, something I even then thought irreverent.

Sometimes I wonder if Jeanie Collins, wherever she is, remembers the solemnity of that moment and if she laughs now at its sententiousness. Perhaps she has forgotten. Or perhaps she shared the elaborate oath with another neighbor or roommate or urchin who struck her fancy.

This, of course, is what I always worried about with best friends -- that my loyalty would not be returned, and, worse, that the ardor of my commitment would be viewed contemptuously, as if it were, like too many of my passions, a bit hysterical in nature.

I suppose what PJ wants out of his best friend is what I wanted, what I still want, which is something between acceptance and beguilement. Nobody wants to be taken for granted by their best friend, yet most of us want our friendships to endure not just the enchantments of our lives, but the unpleasant tedium of them. That may be changing today, as cell phones, e-mail and text messaging allow us to evade the banal dreariness of our chums, checking in only for the juicy bits.

I told PJ about a time when yet another best friend, Julie, seemed to prefer another mutual friend, Susan, to me. Susan had Levi corduroys in every color, a subscription to *Seventeen*, a room of her own and as much Juicy Fruit as she wanted. Who wouldn't want to be best friends with a girl who not only had all of Fleetwood Mac's albums but her own stereo on which to play them? PJ asked me what I did when I suspected that Julie preferred Susan to me. I lied, of course. I told him that mine was a ridiculous suspicion since my charisma was irresistible to Julie, just as his would be to Michael.

In truth, of course, I sulked. I seethed. I sunk into myself, read Charlotte Bronte and nurtured a roiling animus toward Stevie Nicks.

"I do not want people to be very agreeable," Jane Austen wrote, "as it saves me the trouble of liking them a great deal." I yearn for Austen's shimmering self-reliance, her blithe dismissal of a woman's preternatural yearning for a decent, abiding friend. Of course she had sisters, I think. Easy for her to say.

It is hard to tell a 6-year-old that the friend he should value most is his own counsel. It is harder, still, to tell him that integrity of character is its own reward, and that once you have that, your presence becomes electrifying. Only a fool would avoid you. But for now, he is merely a boy with a wounded heart, presuming himself not good enough, marginalized by the one he values most.

It is not enough, I suppose, to tell him I have been where he is, that estrangement is part of the human condition. It is not enough, but it is the truth, and sometimes the truth is the only balm we have.

This Cracker Can Never Get Stale

In Casco Bay, Sunday nights are refreshingly predictable. Most of the 365 brave souls who weather the winter in this intemperate cove of Maine have their dinners in the middle of the day and then, after a full and lazy afternoon, enjoy a late supper of salt fish and Crown Pilot crackers.

Or they did until last June.

Last June, Nabisco took the venerable Crown Pilot crackers off the shelves. Island Market on Chebeague was out of the them. So was Shaw's. And so was Paul's, one of those richly unglamorous places where you can order your groceries and have them arrive by boat in tidy little succulent packages. But no Crown Pilots came from Paul's after Nabisco determined that the crackers, a New England favorite, were a "marginal" seller.

"Nothing like Oreos," said Donna Miller Damon, whose family roots in Casco Bay reach back to 1756. Indeed, Nabisco only sold Crown Pilots in three states: Maine, Massachusetts and New Hampshire. There, the cracker was indispensable to the hardy souls who draw their sustenance from the ocean. Mainers use the Crown Pilot to thicken their chowder and have been doing so since the 19th century.

Next week, Nabisco will hold a press conference at the hub of Boston Harbor to determine the future of Crown Pilot crackers. If the Crown Pilot comes back to new England, it will be a victory for the tenacious Yankees who fought for the cracker. In Casco Bay, they've been waging a campaign to keep the Crown Pilot, and it has picked up enough steam to get the folks at Nabisco to reconsider.

128

"It's been amazing the stories people tell us about how to use the cracker," said Damon, who is organizing the campaign.

"One man told me about how they used to fry clams and then fry the pilot crackers in the fat of the clam left in the pan," Damon said. "My son told me to try it with scallops and I tried soaking them in the fried scallop juice but it wasn't the same. Other people soak them in hot water and put sugar on them and eat them with milk as a dessert."

No, it's not biscotti, but Mainers have simple tastes.

I have simple tastes, too, and I can remember the admirably sturdy maroon box the Crown Pilots came in, the little gold crown over the "O" in the name, the enormous dish of chowder floating off in the background like a dream. Crown Pilots were what my mother used to give me when I was sick in bed with an upset tummy, which was often. Anything with taste made me sick.

"Is that an herb in there," I'd say, suspiciously, eying the Lipton chicken noodle soup.

"It's just parsley; it won't kill you," my mother would say.

But as any picky eater knows, anything that's green and floats is toxic.

Oh, for the Crown Pilot cracker with its rectangular blandness. Like air with geometry. Yes, the Crown Pilot cracker, with its tiny, well-apportioned holes, the wonderfully flat flavor, the utterly prosaic, putty taste of it. The way it broke into your mouth and sent foggy plumes of dust into your every cavity. The way it meshed so perfectly with your saliva, becoming one gluey, cement-like mortar that stuck to the outline of your gums like caulk to a window. The Crown Pilot was the Jimmy Stewart of Crackers; tall and flat, but with a great poignancy to the word "dull."

Those of us who admired its textureless, tasteless character simply swoon at the sight of a Crown Pilot box. I see a box of Crown Pilots and I remember my baby blue, quilted satin robe with the embroidered bunnies on the lapel. I see my 13-inch

Sears black and white TV and the flicker of the mid-day movie, which was the best part about being sick, next to the Crown Pilots, which I consumed fervently all day.

Damon is well aware that there are other crackers out there. Just stop into a grocery store these days. You'd think they would give the cracker aisle its own Interstate. Crackers with cheese; crackers with lemon; flat bread crackers; crackers with low salt, low fat, low sodium...There is a veritable island of crackers to select from today, all of them offering a precious uniqueness. "Choices," my mother says, writing the word out on the paper table cloth of a restaurant with typical dramatic flourish. "That's what's destroying this country today. There are too many damned choices."

As for the new crackers, the islanders have already had their say. "All trendy," said one islander with a Yankee sneer. "Here today, gone tomorrow."

Clearly there are other crackers that can thicken chowder. Oyster crackers, for example, are perfect once you get over the fact that they won't taste remotely like (ugh!) oysters. But Damon says that's not the issue.

"It's the oldest product Nabisco makes," she says. "It makes sense people are going to be connected to it. It's like apple pie. They equate it with memory."

It's a Proustian idea, perhaps, the way the bite of a cracker can send you reeling back to another time, another place, a place sepia with distinction and belonging. But it is true, nonetheless, that the precious nature of a cracker, even a bland cracker, an absolutely ordinary cracker, plucked from the days when there were only three or four crackers to choose from, is grand in its own right. Perhaps it reminds people of their grandmothers, or their grandfathers or of Sunday nights were there was little to do but chew on raw fish and talk to family. Perhaps it reminds us that there was a time when there were few choices. And that given the choice, many of us would rather have that simple, but vanishing, option.

Putting Away The Camera,
And A Part Of A Life

Madame has given up the camera. It is too much. It is not her sight, which remains acute; or her health, which continues to be vigorous; but her spirit, which has seemed to leach away since the death of her husband three years ago.

In truth, Madame, my adoptive French mother, with whom I lived in 1983, has always had a friable spirit, though it took me some time to understand it. When I came to live with them in their tiny stucco house with its steely slate roof and robin's egg blue shutters, she seemed severe, certain, resolute. In retrospect, I see that that may have been my own anxiety. I knew no one in France and the only English the two retirees with whom I was living spoke were a few lines from Cole Porter's "C'est Magnifique."

Maybe I began to suspect when I saw Madame's hands shake while pouring a post-postprandial cup of tea. Or when I saw the regimen of small white pills she furiously took with dinner. Or saw her castigate herself over too-long naps or rub the stump of a pinkie finger severed decades before.

By the time I knew she had suffered several nervous breakdowns, I had already grown hopelessly attached. I should have been just a boarder to Madame and Monsieur, but my vulnerability, coupled with their aesthetic curiosity and puckish affection, knitted us together. Each night I would listen for the quiet knock at my door and Madame's solicitous entreaty, "*Ma cherie? Veux-tu une tasse de the,*" and I would join them in their snug, tidy kitchen to drink bottomless cups of sugary tea, while they spoke about life, the war, and the endlessly variable anecdotes they could coax out of the garden.

One evening about halfway through my stay, Madame alerted me to a documentary on France's Channel 1 about insane asylums. She asked if I would like to join her in the salon to watch it. I said I would. Television was an anomaly in that house; the closest we got to media entertainment was the night we listened to Piaf albums over and over again on the phonograph, staring at the machine as if it would get up and move. It was while watching the documentary with Madame that I understood how close she had come to losing her mind. She shook. Trembled, really, to the point where the sofa on which we were sitting shuddered. I made the mistake of referring to the patients as "*fous,*" literally madmen or lunatics. She reared back and spat out a venomous reply, castigating me for my cruelty and audacity, while I helplessly stammered that my mistake had been borne out of my ineptitude with the language, not ridicule.

People who have not lived among the mentally ill often wrongly assume that there is some specific catalyst for their illness, just as they suspect that depression is a persistent and perpetual state of immobilizing despair. Not always. I knew that Madame had moments of catatonia severe enough to require periodic institutionalization. I never saw those moments. But I saw her close to the edge.

What I felt most was Madame's susceptibility to despair. She seemed to feel life more acutely than normal. I suppose this is what led her to photography. She seemed to see colors more vividly and frame the most ordinary sights into extraordinary aesthetics. In the garden, she could freeze an image of a sparrow alighting on a hollyhock or a lizard sunning itself on the flat leaf of a turnip with unerring fidelity. So often would she describe these visual poetics that I began to feel oafish for passing right by them.

Madame photographed in black and white, because, she said, she loved the subtleties of texture it offered. But I often believed it was because color was so alive that it overwhelmed her. Her hunger to capture the extraordinary grace of the prosaic was consuming. "I have to take a break sometimes," she told me. "It is all too much."

Over the years, through her magical letters and my too brief visits, this black dog of depression has been a pestering and oppressive intrusion. I foolishly and vainly believed a few insightful, loving words would cure, or at least assuage her. I never found them. The dog was always just outside her door.

In her latest letter, she tells me that the city has demolished the building where she and a few other amateurs used to develop their photographs. Just as well, she writes. "It's too complicated and exhausting for me. I cannot do it any more."

But what if what exhausts us sustains us? I worry for Madame, as it seems I always have. What does she do with that searing vision that sees so much in so little?

At the end of the letter, she has created a collage of dried flowers, tender sprouts and candy-colored orange petals. I see them, and I am on the terrace with her in Angers, again, waiting for her razor gaze to direct me to something sublime, almost close enough to touch. Maybe this is the aesthetic life force, or maybe it is what she has been reduced to. It is all she has now, a little slice of beauty to keep the demon dogs at bay.

His Life's Work Offered Shelter From The Cold

The day they mourned the Padre, a thin skein of snow spread over the south end of Waterbury. It was cold.

After he died, an icy gale lashed through the Northeast, sending men like Frank Rotella to the sheltering inlets of drafty old buildings to catch a break. When you are old and homeless and cold, like Rotella, you spend days like this wandering in and out of public buildings and forgotten passageways, the thrum in your head silently ticking off the minutes until you can slip into bed.

Because of the Rev. Philip J. Cascia, Rotella could indulge the dream of sleep. Because of Father Cascia, he had, on a bleak, unforgiving night, a bed. Because of the man they called Padre, Rotella could have a hot meal. Because Philip J. Cascia had a mission, and his mission was here.

"This place is God's gift," said Rotella, a tall, stooped man with a salt-and-pepper beard, sunken cheeks and cataracts veiling his chocolate brown eyes. "The man put his heart and soul into this place. This was his life. He took advantage of his gift and he convinced people who were doing good to build this place, because, but for the grace of God, they could have been in here."

The Rev. Philip J. Cascia, who died Tuesday and will be buried today, spoke with heads of state, presidents and tyrants, popes and papal nuncios, but his heart was always here -- in the south end of Waterbury, a place that has the gritty, barren feel of used-to-bes and could-haves. The St. Vincent DePaul Shelter, which Cascia began in 1984, is now the largest in the state, with 126 beds. It houses guys with bad luck, drifters with sick minds and little boys and girls with no place else to go.

"If you lay down in the cold weather like this, you die," says William James Goss, perched alone at the end of a bench in the shelter's dining area. "You have to keep walking. Find a spot, walk in a circle. Because if you lie down, you die." Goss never knew Cascia. "I wish I had met the man," says Goss, sitting under a photograph of Cascia with former President Reagan. "Because if it weren't for him, more people would be dying."

"The poor you will always have with you," Jesus said, and the poor were always with Father Cascia. The year after he was ordained, nervy and too bold for his own good, he told then-archbishop John Francis Whealon he was bored. Flippantly, the archbishop told him, "Well, go help the poor in Waterbury."

Poverty is an intractable and elusive beast but Cascia did his best to slay it. He was not a magician or a saint, but if he did anything miraculous it was to convince people with a light within them to join him on his quest.

"When you entered into his presence, he made you feel like you knew him all your life," said his long-time friend Paul Iadorola, executive director of the St. Vincent DePaul Society. "Once you got through that, you found yourself working for him. You'd do anything for him."

"He'd tell you to hop on one foot and you'd do it and you never knew why," said Pat Hollmann, of the shelter. "This was his mission."

People who knew Father Cascia talk about the dichotomy between the erudite homilist whose sermons wormed their way indelibly into their minds, and the smart-aleck jokester who was the first one at the party to pick up his Jack Daniels, cigar and microphone and begin to sing.

"He used to say to me, 'George, guess who was asking for you?'" recalled his long-time deacon George Dingle. "I'd say, 'Who?' And he'd say, 'Nobody,' and we'd laugh like heck."

The man nominated for a Nobel Peace Prize for his work bringing international sports teams together, spent his Friday nights on Baldwin Street in Waterbury, handing out food and bestowing blessings.

"He was most happy when he was with the kids and with the homeless," said Iadarola. "He loved the guys down there."

Friday night, Hollmann, tall and angular and wan from a tenacious cold, walked a plastic plate of chocolate cookies to the center of the shelter's dining area. "Kids," she said, waving toward half-dozen children. "Cookies." Hesitantly, the children, coats unzipped, mucus running down their noses, put down their crayons and paper airplanes and gently devoured the chocolate treats.

"This man was, above anything else, a priest," said Mary Mauriello, long-time director of the shelter. "Everything was either right or wrong with him. He saw something that needed to be done. He didn't hold a hundred meetings. He decided we needed a homeless shelter. He got busy and he did it. Not a finer priest ever existed."

But bad luck does not spare good men and so it was that Father Cascia was felled by a rare and aggressive form of lymphoma, treated with a heavy barrage of chemotherapy. He was angry at the diagnosis. Then accepting, and finally, last December, so thankful, he planned a Mass of Thanksgiving. He never lived to celebrate it. "You do not get justice in this world," he had told his friend and parishioner Frank Travisano some years before. "Only charity begets justice."

On a Friday night in a brick building on a forgotten street in Waterbury, a few men, women and children got justice. They got a warm meal, a shower, and a place to lay their heads. It is not a job.

It is not a paycheck. It is not a house. It is not love. But it is something like it. When, today, they lay Father Philip J. Cascia in the ground, a stranger will sleep in a warm place. And Father Cascia will rest in peace.

ABOUT THE AUTHOR

Graduated *magna cum laude* from American University, O'Shaughnessy, a native of Massachusetts, is a graduate of Wesleyan and American Universities. Following college, O'Shaughnessy worked at Gannett News Service in Washington, D.C., the *Norwich Bulletin* in Connecticut and the *Almanac Newspapers* in Potomac, Md.

photo by Alan Bisbort

She studied both writing and theology at Georgetown University. Her freelance work has appeared in *Connecticut Magazine*, the *Washington Post* and *Wesleyan Magazine*.

In 1992, Tracey O'Shaughnessy's by-line began appearing in the *Republican-American* in Waterbury, Connecticut, and quickly attracted a local following. As her deeply informed eloquence and generosity of spirit took root in weekly columns, feature articles, art reviews and social commentary, that readership grew regionally. Then, as the awards started pouring in, she gained a national following. Now, with the advent of the Internet, readers from around the world have found her. The Associate Features Editor of the *Republican-American*, she still writes regularly about family life, religion, society and culture.

Her writings have won praise from the American Society of Newspaper Editors, the New England Associated Press News Executives Association, the American Academy of Religion and the American Association of Sunday and Features Editors. Her "Sunday Reflections" column -- many installments of which appear in this volume -- was singled out for the prestigious Wilbur Award by the Religion Communicators Council in both 2001 and 2003; and earned awards in 2005 and 2006 for Best Opinion Writing on Religion Award from the American Academy of Religion. She has won a Clarion Award for her writing on women, and her work has also won numerous top honors from the New England Associated Press News Executives. Most recently, she received the 2008 Missouri Lifestyle Journalism Award.

She is married to the writer Alan Bisbort and lives with their son, PJ, and dog, Calvin, in Cheshire, Connecticut.